体育英语专业系列教材

总主编 田 慧

综合英语教程
AN INTEGRATED ENGLISH COURSE

(第一册)

主　编：柳莉蕊
副主编：李　晶

编　委：孙曙光　　王　严　　崔珣丽　赵　雪
　　　　周春红　　李海英　　袁　哲　张西环
　　　　韩亚辉　　宋玉梅
审　校：田　慧　Carol Griffiths　Vera Lee

北京大学出版社
PEKING UNIVERSITY PRESS

图书在版编目（CIP）数据

综合英语教程 .1/ 田慧总主编 . —北京：北京大学出版社，2008.10
（体育英语专业系列教材）
ISBN 978-7-301-14274-5

Ⅰ. 综… Ⅱ. 田… Ⅲ. 体育－英语－高等学校－教材 Ⅳ. H31

中国版本图书馆 CIP 数据核字 (2008) 第 146499 号

书　　名	综合英语教程（第一册） ZONGHE YINGYU JIAOCHENG (DI-YI CE)
著作责任者	田　慧　总主编
责任编辑	徐万丽
标准书号	ISBN 978-7-301-14274-5
出版发行	北京大学出版社
地　　址	北京市海淀区成府路 205 号　100871
网　　址	http://www.pup.cn
电　　话	邮购部 010-62752015　发行部 010-62750672　编辑部 010-62759634
电子信箱	zln0120@163.com
印刷者	北京虎彩文化传播有限公司
经销者	新华书店 787 毫米 ×1092 毫米　16 开本　12.5 印张　238 千字 2008 年 10 月第 1 版　2020 年 9 月第 3 次印刷
定　　价	28.00 元（配有光盘）

未经许可，不得以任何方式复制或抄袭本书之部分或全部内容。
版权所有，侵权必究
举报电话：010-62752024　电子信箱：fd@pup.pku.edu.cn
图书如有印装质量问题，请与出版部联系，电话：010-62756370

前　言

　　从2002年开始,国内的体育院校纷纷开设了体育英语专业,培养在体育领域从事对外交流工作的国际体育人才。经过5年多的发展,体育英语专业既显示出强大的生机和活力,又面临着诸多困难,首要的问题就是教材问题。目前,体育英语专业大多在技能类课程,特别是基础阶段课程中沿用了全国统编英语专业教材。这些教材选材精当、设计合理,对夯实学生语言基本功起到巨大作用,但针对性不强,未能体现出本专业的特色。因此,从2004年开始,我们就着手策划编写一套供体育英语专业学生使用的系列教材,并于2007年获得北京高等教育精品教材建设立项项目。此系列教材包括基础阶段的《综合英语教程》、《英语听说教程》、《英语阅读教程》和高级阶段的《体育英语阅读》等,首批推出的是基础阶段的《综合英语教程》和《英语听说教程》。

　　经教育部批准的《高等学校英语专业英语教学大纲》指出:英语专业学生应具有扎实的语言基本功、宽广的知识面、一定的相关专业知识、较强的能力和较高的素质。基础阶段的各教程正是按照这一培养目标编写的,立足于加强学生语言基本功,在培养语言基本功的同时渗透体育元素、人文精神,以提高学生的体育知识水平和人文素养,并在设计中力图培养学生的跨文化交际能力和独立思维能力。同时,本系列教材的一个突出特点是将各门课程的同一单元统一于一个话题,学生在综合英语、英语阅读、英语听说中同步围绕一个话题进行不同的技能训练,也使得他们能从不同角度认识同一问题。

　　《综合英语教程》是为第一、二学年的专业基础教学配备的课本,训练听、说、读、写、译等各方面技能。教程没有将语法和语言功能作为编写主线,而是以课文的主题和内容作为编写的基础;每一单元围绕同一主题选编了两篇文章,并将有关的体育内容穿插其中。Text I 作为主课文,教师课堂精讲,并处理与课文相关的课文理解、词汇、翻译等练习;Text II 是对该单元话题的扩展和深化,只配课文理解练习和话题讨论,目的在于开拓学生思路,就相关问题提出自己的观点和见解,从而培养学生分析问题和解决问题的能力。课文后设计了综合能力训练和口语活动及写作练习,进一步巩固该单元的知识,加强语言应用能力,同时为参加全国英语专业四级考试做准备。通过每个单元的两篇课文的学习和各种练习,学生可对单元话题的认识加深,在掌握语言知识、加强语言技能的基础上,还能就话题进行口头、笔头交流,陈述观点,发表意见。

本教程课文大都选自英美原文,为了方便教学个别地方我们做了删节和微小的改动。在选材时,我们注重体育专业与人文通识并重,注重内容的专业性和人文性,在英语学习中既学到体育知识,又增加人文知识,提高人文素养。有关体育方面的课文均选自国外的体育教科书,有极强的针对性。

《综合英语教程(第一册)》共12单元,供体育英语专业一年级第一学期教学使用。按照综合英语课程每学期96学时的教学时数,每单元需用8学时完成教学,各校在使用时也可以根据需要进行调整。

编纂过程中,外籍专家 Vera Lee、Carol Griffiths、Susan Lee、Albert Kaan 都先后编写或改写了部分课文,在此谨表谢忱。教程选材过程中,参阅选编了大量英美国家报纸杂志和有关教科书,在此谨向原著者致以谢意。

北京体育大学外语系承担了本系列教材的编写工作。由于经验和水平限制,书中不当之处在所难免,敬请使用本教程的师生批评指正。

本教程编写完成之际,正当北京奥运会开幕前夕,欣逢盛世,相信2008年奥运会后,我国的体育事业必将迎来一个崭新的发展机遇期,对外交流也会日益扩大。随着全球化的不断深入,国际体育交往愈发凸显其重要性,中国亟需引进国外先进的体育科学理论、训练方法、休闲理念和健康的生活方式。我们期待,本套教材能对提高我国体育英语专业的建设水平,培养更多的国际体育人才,进而提高我国的体育发展水平贡献绵薄之力。

编者

2008 年 7 月

TABLE OF CONTENTS

Unit 1　Strategies 1
　　　　Text I　Sun Tzu: Strategies for the Twenty-first Century / 1
　　　　Text II　On the Ball / 10

Unit 2　Olympics 16
　　　　Text I　Olympics through History—Peace through Competition / 16
　　　　Text II　Barcelona 1992—The Games of the XXVIth Olympiad / 30

Unit 3　Education 36
　　　　Text I　Lifelong Learning / 36
　　　　Text II　Angels on a Pin / 46

Unit 4　Manners 53
　　　　Text I　Mind Your Manners / 53
　　　　Text II　My Chinese Canadian Family / 63

Unit 5　Leisure and Sports 70
　　　　Text I　Game / 70
　　　　Text II　Leisure-time Activities—Picture and Sound / 79

Unit 6　Happiness 85
　　　　Text I　The Science of Happiness / 86
　　　　Text II　Ten Keys to Happiness / 94

Unit 7　Dreams 101
　　　　Text I　Creating Your Dreams / 101
　　　　Text II　The Manifest and Latent Meaning of Dreams / 111

Unit 8　Hobbies ··· **117**
　　　　Text I　Favorite Hobby—Reading / 117
　　　　Text II　Discover Why Knitting Is a Great and Timeless Hobby
　　　　　　　　That You Can Benefit from / 125

Unit 9　Relationships ·· **130**
　　　　Text I　Good Coach-Athlete Relationship through Message-Sending
　　　　　　　　Systems / 130
　　　　Text II　The Story of My Life / 144

Unit 10　Festival ··· **151**
　　　　Text I　The 4th of July—a Day of Rejoicing / 151
　　　　Text II　Father's Day / 160

Unit 11　Food ··· **166**
　　　　Text I　How Americans Eat and Drink / 166
　　　　Text II　Fast-food Fix / 173

Unit 12　Media ··· **179**
　　　　Text I　British Newspapers and Magazines / 179
　　　　Text II　The Formative Years of Sports Television / 188

References ·· **194**

Unit 1 Strategies

Warm-up Activities

1. What are some of your study habits? How did they evolve? Which worked best or worst?
2. Studying a second language can be a challenge for most students. Suppose you are a student who handles this challenge with great success. You are asked to make a presentation of effective learning strategies.

Text I

Sun Tzu: Strategies for the Twenty-first Century

Pre-reading Questions

1. Have you ever heard of Sun Tzu?
2. Do you know or can you guess what he might be famous for?

1   Sun Tzu was a Chinese general who lived around 500 B.C. Not much is known about him personally, however, his legacy remains in the form of a collection of essays known as *The Art of War*. In these essays, Sun Tzu explains the strategies which he believes are essential for military success, for instance, that victory is based on deception. Another key strategic principle advocated by Sun Tzu was that it is best to win battles without fighting. In the years since *The Art of War* was written, the principles contained in its pages have been applied to many different contexts, such as sport and academic study.

2   Awareness of Sun Tzu's ideas first reached the west towards the end of the eighteenth century by means of a translation by the French Jesuit priest, Father Amiot. In the 1970s, the American diplomat Henry Kissinger revived interest in *The Art of War* which has since been frequently cited in contemporary books on diplomacy and business. Although Sun Tzu's principles originally related to war, in fact much of his writing relates to interpersonal dynamics which can be applied to any area of human endeavour.

3   Although the original connotation of strategy was warlike and aggressive, as applied to learning the focus is on the achievement of success. Applied specifically to learning language, the term strategy might be defined as activities consciously chosen by learners for the purpose of regulating their own learning. According to this definition, strategies are active steps which students take in order to regulate or take charge of their own learning. Strategies are goal-oriented and purposeful rather than vague and directionless, and students deliberately choose these activities for themselves in rather than waiting passively for others (perhaps teachers) to suggest or impose them.

4   Because they were originally conceived with a military purpose in mind, not all of Sun Tsu's principles can be applied to a learning context. Some, however, are very appropriate for modern students. Sun Tsu's ideas on the importance of planning are an example of strategies with contemporary relevance for today's language students. According to Sun Tzu, planning represents a road to either success or ruin. Nevertheless, he points out that we should not be inflexible, but prepared to modify our plans as circumstances dictate. As water shapes its course according to the ground over which it runs, so should we be prepared to adapt according to the circumstances we encounter rather than rigidly persevering with pre-determined plans which are proving unproductive. We should also be prepared to use strategies in combination. Sun Tzu likens the combining of strategies to music. Although there are only five basic notes, when combined, they can create more melodies than can ever be heard.

Unit 1　Strategies

5　　　Potentially, there are a huge number of strategies which students might choose in order to facilitate their progress towards their language learning goal. According to recent research, successful language learners have large strategy repertoires of which they make frequent use. Successful students are especially aware of the need to use strategies to expand their vocabulary: it would seem to be common sense that, without the appropriate words, it is difficult to say much in a new language. However, it is also important to know how to put the words together (grammar), and successful students are aware of this too. Successful learners use all four skills to develop their linguistic capabilities: for instance, they write letters, they listen to radio and native speakers, they talk to shopkeepers or taxi drivers, and, perhaps most important, they read in the target language. By means of reading, they encounter new lexical items, they are exposed to a model of how language is used, and they obtain cultural information. Furthermore, books are patient: they can be re-read any number of times until comprehension is secured, whereas real-life interlocutors can become irritated, resulting in loss of confidence and motivation on the part of the struggling student.

6　　　Students who use the kinds of strategies noted above are likely to be successful language learners, but they must be prepared to be pro-active, persistent and hard-working. Learning a new language is not easy, but for those who are prepared to work hard, strategies used flexibly and in combination are likely to be of great assistance. As Sun Tzu points out, there are only five primary colours (which he lists as red, yellow, blue, white and black), but, in combination, they create more hues than we can ever see. Likewise there are only five cardinal tastes (sour, acrid, salty, sweet and bitter), yet, when combined, they produce more flavours than we can ever savour. And so it is with language learning strategies: when used in effective combinations, they become a powerful weapon which successful students use in order to win the battle to learn language.

(803 words)

Words and Expressions

legacy	/ˈleɡəsɪ/	n.	something handed down from an ancestor or a predecessor or from the past 遗产
strategy	/ˈstrætɪdʒɪ/	n.	a detailed plan for achieving success in situations such as war, politics, business, industry or sport 策略，计谋
essential	/ɪˈsenʃəl/	adj.	necessary; basic or indispensable 必需的；基本的
deception	/dɪˈsepʃən/	n.	a ruse; a trick 诈术；诡计
advocate	/ˈædvəkɪ(eɪ)t/	vt.	to publicly support or suggest an idea, development or way of doing something 拥护；提倡；主张
diplomat	/ˈdɪpləmæt/	n.	an official whose job is to represent a government in its relations with other governments 外交官
revive	/rɪˈvaɪv/	vt.	to bring back to life or consciousness 使复活
contemporary	/kənˈtempərərɪ/	adj.	current; modern 当代的；现代的
interpersonal	/ˌɪntəˈpɜːsənl/	adj.	connected with relationships between people 人与人之间的；人际关系的
dynamics	/daɪˈnæmɪks/	n.	the social, intellectual, or moral forces that produce activity and change 动态
endeavour	/ɪnˈdevə/	n.	an attempt to do something 努力，尽力
connotation	/ˌkɒnəʊˈteɪʃən/	n.	an idea or meaning suggested by or associated with a word or thing 含义
aggressive	/əˈɡresɪv/	adj.	behaving in an angry, threatening way, as if you want to fight or attack someone 侵略性的；攻击性的
deliberately	/dɪˈlɪbərətlɪ/	adv.	carefully and often slowly 深思熟虑地；慎重地
conceive	/kənˈsiːv/	vt.	to form or develop in the mind 构思
ruin	/ˈruːɪn/	n.	total destruction 毁坏；毁灭
modify	/ˈmɒdɪfaɪ/	vt.	to change in form or character; alter 更改；修改
liken sb/sth to sb/sth			to say that someone is similar to or has the same qualities as someone else 把……比作……
facilitate	/fəˈsɪlɪteɪt/	vt.	to make easy or easier 使容易；使便利
expose sb to sth			to make it likely that someone will experience something 使……接触
interlocutor	/ˌɪntəˈlɒkjʊtə/	n.	someone who is involved in a conversation 对话者，谈话者
cardinal	/ˈkɑːdɪnəl/	adj.	very important or basic 基本的，最重要的

Unit 1 Strategies

Reading Comprehension

I. **Write down the sentence or the key words that best sum up the main idea in each paragraph.**

Para. 1 _____

_____

Para. 2 _____

_____

Para. 3 _____

_____

Para. 4 _____

_____

Para. 5 _____

_____

Para. 6 _____

_____

II. **Answer the following questions orally.**
1. In Sun Tzu's essays, what is the most important factor for military success?
2. What is the original connotation of strategy?
3. Can strategies be applied to learning a language? If so, how do you define the term strategy in this field?
4. According to Sun Tzu, what is the significance of planning? Should planning be flexible or inflexible? Explain with examples.
5. How do successful language learners use strategies in their language learning process?
6. Should language learners focus on one language learning strategy or use strategies in combination? Why?

III. **Judge, according to the text, whether the following statements are true or false. For false statements, write the facts in parentheses.**
1. Sun Tzu believed that strategies were necessary for winning battles.
(   )

2. People's interest in *The Art of War* was aroused by the American diplomat Henry Kissinger because he translated it.
   (   )
3. Students apply strategies to learning language in order to regulate and facilitate their own learning.
   (   )
4. Because Sun Tzu's strategies were originally related to war, not all apply to facilitating students' learning.
   (   )
5. Language learners should focus on one language learning strategy in order to make full use of it.
   (   )
6. Students who use the kinds of strategies mentioned in paragraph 5 are always successful.
   (   )

IV. Paraphrase, use your own words to explain the sentences in the text with the help of the context.

1. (Para. 1) Not much is known about him personally, however, his legacy remains in the form of a collection of essays known as *The Art of War*.

2. (Para. 2) Although Sun Tzu's principles originally related to war, in fact much of his writing relates to interpersonal dynamics which can be applied to any area of human endeavour.

3. (Para. 3) Applied specifically to learning language, the term strategy might be defined as activities consciously chosen by learners for the purpose of regulating their own learning.

4. (Para. 4) As water shapes its course according to the ground over which it runs, so should we be prepared to adapt according to the circumstances we

encounter rather than rigidly persevering with pre-determined plans which are proving unproductive.

_____

_____

5. (Para. 5) Furthermore, books are patient: they can be re-read any number of times until comprehension is secured, whereas real-life interlocutors can become irritated, resulting in loss of confidence and motivation on the part of the struggling student.

_____

_____

Vocabulary Exercises

I. **Fill in each blank with one of the given words and note the difference of meaning between them. Change the form when necessary.**

1. EXPOSE   IMPOSE
   A. This program will _____ burdens on all of us in order to increase our production.
   B. His companions have threatened to _____ his crime to the police.
   C. Travel around the world _____ children to different languages and cultures.
   D. New duties will be _____ on wines and spirits in the next year.

2. LEGACY   HERITAGE   INHERITANCE
   A. Mr. Jones received his house by _____.
   B. Disease and famine are often _____ of war.
   C. The _____ of moral uprightness has been passed down from generation to generation among Chinese people.
   D. The poets in the 18th century left us great literary _____.

3. CONCEIVE   PERCEIVE
   A. I couldn't _____ the meaning of his words.
   B. The study of an academic discipline alters the way we _____ the world.
   C. It was said that scientists first _____ the idea of the atomic bomb in

the 1930s.

 D. To the elderly, the past is often _____ to be better than the present.

4. CAPABILITY CAPACITY

 A. The newly-built hall has a _____ of 1,000 people.

 B. Shirley has a good knowledge of English, but simultaneous interpretation is beyond her _____ .

 C. A willingness and a _____ to change are necessary to be successful in a market-oriented economy.

 D. Children's _____ for learning is infinite.

II. **Choose a word or phrase that best completes each of the following sentences.**

1. Shop assistants should _____ to give the customers satisfaction.
 A. endure B. endeavour C. endow D. engage

2. Foreigners may invest in most sectors, _____ public services, without prior approval.
 A. rather than B. other than C. besides D. instead of

3. Their relationship was _____ mutual respect.
 A. based in B. base for C. based upon D. on the base of

4. It does not apply _____ domestic consumers.
 A. in B. to C. with D. for

5. The fire _____ damage to their property.
 A. due to B. resulted from C. resulted in D. owing to

III. **Fill in the blank in each sentence with a word taken from the box in its appropriate form.**

create	persevere	aggressive	conscious
specify	apply	modify	persist
diplomat	origin	aware	expose

1. Have you filled in the _____ form for your passport yet?

2. The _____ of the minister's love affair forced him to resign.

3. For most people, the main question about genetically _____ food is: Do I have to eat it?

4. Can you be more _____ about where your back hurts?

Unit 1   Strategies

5. A good parliamentarian must have an _____ of what the people at home want.
6. What they fear most is our resolute _____ in our demands.
7. The two countries established _____ relations last year.
8. This painting is a copy; the _____ is in Paris.
9. Television violence can encourage _____ in children.
10. He lost _____ after his accident and never regained it.
11. Our education must provide knowledge and nurture _____ .
12. The reason for failure in most cases is lack of _____ .

Translation Exercises

Translate each of the following sentences into English, using the word or phrase given in the brackets.

1. 水和阳光是植物赖以生存的元素。(be essential for)

2. 这部电影根据真实故事改编,非常感人。(be based on)

3. 你目前的心境是否与童年的遭遇有关? (to relate to)

4. 我们应把科技资源应用于社会生活的每一个领域。(apply to)

5. 过去人们常常通过信件进行远距离沟通,而现在我们可以通过网络来传递信息了。(by means of)

6. 苏珊成功的秘诀告诉我们:在工作中要积极进取而不是消极等待成功。(rather than)

7. 老板出差期间让她负责办公室事务,她欣然答应了。(take charge of)

8. 公司正在联合几家海外合伙人研制新产品,并有望年底在市场销售。(in combination with)

Text II

On the Ball

> *Pre-reading Questions*
> 1. Is there something unusual about the picture?
> 2. What do you think the story is going to be about?

1   People often ask me what kind of sports I like to play and my response has been the same since I can remember: soccer, street hockey, and pretty much anything that involves a ball. I love sports but if there was one I pursued more than any other it would be soccer. At this point it should be noted that what North Americans call soccer other countries call football; what I call football would be American football, a totally different sport.

Vera puts her best foot forward

2   Before developing into my current state as a soccer player, I first needed to get over one obstacle: I was a girl. Fortunately growing up in the 80s I didn't encounter too much gender inequality as compared to earlier decades, or previous centuries for that matter, but there was still a stigma for girls playing sports, especially "boys' sports". I wanted to prove to other people that girls were just as skillful at kicking a ball as boys.

3   My early days playing soccer were with the boys during recess time. As the only girl playing, I was naturally picked last when the teams were divided. However, I knew I was better than they thought and just needed to prove myself. My goal was to first improve my dribbling and ball handling skills. I carefully observed how the boys would deke around me like a pylon. I asked my neighbour to teach me some tricks of his own and I practiced those skills until I perfected them. Then during our recess games, I would pull those tricks from out of my sleeves and impress everyone. It worked. Subsequently, I was not

chosen last anymore but second-last, a step in the right direction. Not long afterwards I moved up the ranks.

As I entered high school, soccer games became more competitive as school pride was added to the mix. I wasn't playing pick-up games anymore but actually had to train, practice, and prepare weeks in advance before meeting the opponents. This was the big leagues now.

To outlast the other team we needed to be in tip-top shape. Physical endurance and stamina is a major part of the game so after going out on many jogs and running numerous sprints, we as a team would be physically ready. To outplay the other team we worked on different skills and strategies by doing simulation drills, games such as three on two, where to stand and what to do during corner kicks and throw-ins.

We also worked on communication skills on the field, for example by calling out "Man-on!" when there was someone coming to take the ball, or "Support!" to let teammates know they could pass the ball back. To outsmart the other team we needed to anticipate what would happen next. The defensive strategy was to always "stick to your man", to cover them and make sure they weren't open to receive the ball. The game plan was simple: get to the ball first before the opponent.

Watching videos of professional soccer teams also taught us how the professionals played the game. It gave us some insights on the many different tactics we could put into our game play as well. The day before each game I would become very excited and would make up scenarios in my mind and imagine how I would do give-and-go passes, deke around my opponents and score. I would put on my team uniform and picture myself on the field, mentally preparing how I would deal with each passing situation.

This visualization technique was also used when I coached a girls' high school soccer team. Many players were nervous and uptight for fear of performing badly. To calm their anxiety, I had them sit down and close their eyes, take a few deep breaths, and talked them through an imaginary situation on the field. I told them that so long as they give their best effort, then they have already played successfully. Not only did this imagery help them prepare mentally for the game, but it also helped them to relax and reminded them to have fun.

Soccer has always been an exciting sport to play, the pace of the game, the quick thinking involved, the variables of where the ball can end up. How well a

team can control the ball or what strategies they put into practice during the game to control the ball is half the fun. The other half is simply just playing with your friends.

(760 words)

Reading Comprehension

I. Answer the following questions with the information you got from the passage.
   1. Why did the author emphasize the ball game she played was soccer, not American football?
   2. What obstacles did the author have to overcome before she became a soccer player? How did she get over them?
   3. According to the text, what kinds of training and skills are required for a soccer team to outplay its opponents?
   4. Why has soccer always been an exciting sport to play according to the author?

II. Topics for discussion and reflection.
   1. Do you think girls can also be very successful at "boys' sports"? If you think so, can you provide some good examples to support your opinion?
   2. Discuss with your partners whether there is sex discrimination in sports.

Exercises for Integrated Skills

I. Dictation

   Listen to the following passage. Altogether the passage will be read to you four times. During the first reading, which will be read at normal speed, listen and try to understand the meaning. For the second and third readings, the passage will be read sentence by sentence, or phrase by phrase, with intervals of 15 to 20 seconds. The last reading will be done at normal speed again and during this time you should check your work. You will then be given 2 minutes to check through your work once more.

Unit 1 Strategies

II. Cloze

Fill in each blank in the passage below with a word taken from the box in its appropriate form.

meaning	interest	exact	active
communicate	discover	correct	regular
pattern	similar	independent	purpose
mistake	show	conclusion	

What does a successful language learner do? Language learning research ___1___ that successful language learners are ___2___ in many ways.

First of all, successful language learners are ___3___ learners. They do not depend on the book or the teacher; they ___4___ their own ways to learn the language. Instead of waiting for the teacher to explain, they try to find the ___5___ and the rules for themselves. They are good guessers who look for clues and form their own ___6___. When they guess wrong, they guess again. They try to learn from their ___7___.

Successful language learning is ___8___ learning. Therefore, successful learners do not wait for a chance to use the language; they look for such chances. They find people who speak the language and they ask these people to ___9___ them when they make mistakes. They will try anything to ___10___. They are not afraid to repeat what they hear or to say strange things; they are willing to make mistakes and try again. When communication is difficult, they can accept information that is ___11___ or incomplete. It is more important for them to learn to think in the language than to know the ___12___ of every word.

Finally, successful language learners are learners with a ___13___. They want to learn the language because they are ___14___ in the language and the people who speak it. It is necessary for them to learn the language in order to communicate with these people and to learn from them. They find it easy to practice using the language ___15___ because they want to learn with it.

Oral Activities

Activity One

1. Do you have your own learning strategies? In groups, discuss the different learning strategies and then introduce one effective method to other groups.
2. What are the styles of writing in Texts I and II? How do the authors employ the language to suit the styles?

Activity Two

Vocabulary Learning Strategies

For language learners, there are various strategies to learn new vocabulary and each strategy has its own advantage. What is your way to learn new words? Which strategy do you prefer and why? You will be given 2 minutes to memorize the following words and then you will be given a vocabulary test. You may use your own strategies to memorize the words.

animosity	*n.*	hostility, ill will
feasible	*adj.*	capable of being done
agitate	*v.*	to excite, to disturb, to stir up
predecessor	*n.*	a person who has previously occupied a position that another has taken over
credulous	*adj.*	too ready to believe; willing to believe or trust too readily
formulate	*v.*	to prepare from a set of steps (formula), to devise

What was your result in the vocabulary test? Did your strategy help you remember those words? Now discuss with your group members and exchange the strategies you used in the vocabulary test. Report to the rest of the class on different vocabulary learning strategies employed in your group.

Unit 1 Strategies

Writing Practice

Note Writing: Note to Keep in Touch with a Friend

After the crucial college entrance exam, you are a first-year English major in Beijing Sport University. Write a note to your friend, Li Ming, informing him of your new address and asking him to keep in touch with you. You should write in about 60 words.

```
                                              September _____
Li Ming,



                                                       Wang Lei
```

Passage Writing:

Strategies are goal-oriented and purposeful. Have you ever used a strategy to solve your problems and achieve your goals successfully in your life? It can be a strategy in language learning, sports games, speaking contests or intercommunication with people. Write a short passage of around 200 words relating your experience of using strategies in your life.

Unit 2 Olympics

Warm-up Activities

1. Why do you think most athletes dream of participating in the Olympics? Give 4–5 different reasons (for themselves, for the family, for other people, for the nation, and so on).
2. Familiarize yourself with the various Olympic events and present one event to the class (including where it takes place, what equipment is needed and some general rules).

Text I

Olympics through History — Peace through Competition

Pre-reading Questions

1. What are your favorite events at the Olympic Games?
2. Who are your Olympic heroes and why?

1   From the beginning, the purpose of the Olympic Games was to gather together people from different cities, nations and countries to promote peace. Although the Games have evolved over the centuries, politics have always played a crucial role in the success of the peace process and the ultimate success of the Games. The history of the Games has shown us that the attempt to gain political advantage through athletic excellence and competition has not changed with the passage of time.

2   The first record of the Olympic Games being held was in 776 B.C. at the Sanctuary of Zeus at Olympia, named after Mt. Olympus. Dominated by the

temple of Zeus, the ancient stadium of Olympia could accommodate more than 40,000 spectators. This temple was set on the highest mountain in mainland Greece, and in Greek mythology, was believed to be the home of the greatest of the Greek gods and goddesses. In the seventh century B.C. fierce battles were fought for control over the sanctuary where the Games were to take place because with the Games came prestige, economic advantages and political influence.

Mount Olympus in Greece

3   Initially, only amateur male athletes took part in the Games, merely representing their hometowns and earning "bragging rights." Participants were often visitors who happened to be in Olympia at the time of the festival and who were encouraged to compete. During the ancient Games, the competition consisted of running a distance of approximately 192 meters, called the stadion. The first recorded champion of the Olympics was Coroebus, a cook from the nearby city of Elis. At the official award ceremony, on the last day of the Games, the name of the Olympic champion, his father's name, and his homeland would be called out by a Greek judge who would place the sacred olive tree wreath on the winner's head. Although seemingly simple compared to the award ceremonies held in modern Olympics, the participants stood in the temple of Zeus with great pride in their accomplishment.

4   The persistence of battles in Greece eventually led to the enforcement of the Olympic Truce. A treaty signed by three kings, the Truce would allow the athletes, their families, artists, ordinary pilgrims, and diplomats to travel in safety to participate in or attend the Olympic Games. These freed travelers from being pressed into fighting local battles en route to the competition and ensured that the Games would proceed successfully. The Olympic Games reached the height of their popularity between the fifth and the fourth centuries B.C. Thereafter they became more and more professional until, in the Roman period, they provoked much censure. They were eventually discontinued by the Christian Emperor Theodosius I of Rome, who, at the end of the fourth century A.D., condemned them as a pagan spectacle.

5   In 1894 the Olympic Games were revived, largely due to the passion and commitment of a Frenchman named Baron Pierre de Coubertin. He believed that international competition between amateur athletes would help to promote friendly relationships between people from different countries. In the face of strong opposition, in 1894 he assembled 79 delegates from 12 countries to attend the international congress for the re-establishment of the Olympics, and it was decided that the first modern games would be held in Athens in 1896.

6   The 1896 Games in Greece were a tremendous success, with the original Olympic medals being silver and only awarded to the winner of the event. Unfortunately, the next two Olympics, held in Paris and St. Louis, were overshadowed by the Paris Universal Exhibition and the Louisiana Purchase Exposition. In 1908, London hosted a very successful and well-organized event. The International Olympic Committee (IOC) decided to award medals to the top three competitors for the Games and this tradition still holds today. In 1912, at the Stockholm Games, electrical timing equipment was used for the first time in running events. Since 1896, only the onset of WWI and WWII has prevented the Olympic Games from being held. Since the revival of the Olympics in 1894, the numbers of entrants, competing nations and events have increased steadily.

7   Traditionally the competition for the Olympic Games only included limited events in the areas of track and field, which include the decathlon and heptathlon. However, a host of games and sports have been added to reflect the changes in society—archery, badminton, baseball, softball, basketball, boxing, canoeing, kayaking, cycling, diving, equestrian events, fencing, field hockey, gymnastics, judo, taekwondo, the modern pentathlon, rowing, sailing, shooting, soccer, swimming, table tennis, team (field) handball, tennis, trampoline, triathlon, volleyball, water polo, weight lifting, and wrestling. Olympic events for women made their first appearance in 1912. A separate series of winter Olympic meets, inaugurated in 1924 at Chamonix in France, now includes ice hockey, curling, bobsledding, luge, skeleton, skiing, snowboarding, and skating events. Since 1994 the Winter Games have been held in even-numbered years in which the Summer Games are not contested. Until late in the 20th century the modern Olympics were open only to amateurs, but the governing bodies of several sports now permit professionals to compete as well.

8   As a visible focus of world energies, the Olympics have been the victim of many factors that have thwarted the ideals of world cooperation and athletic

excellence. As in ancient Greece, nationalistic fervor has fostered intense rivalries that at times have threatened the very survival of the Games. Although officially only individuals win Olympic medals, nations routinely assign political significance to the feats of their citizens and teams. Between 1952 and 1988 rivalry between the United States and the Soviet Union, rooted in mutual political antagonism, resulted in each boycotting the Games hosted by the other (Moscow, 1980; Los Angeles, 1984). Politics have also influenced the Olympic Games in other ways, from the propaganda of the Nazis in Berlin (1936) to pressures leading to the exclusion of white-ruled Rhodesia from the Munich Games (1972). In Munich, nine Israeli athletes were kidnapped and murdered by Palestinian terrorists.

9   In addition to having to cope with political pressures, the International Olympic Committee, which sets and enforces Olympic policy, has struggled with the licensing and commercialization of the Games and the need to schedule events to accommodate American television networks (whose broadcasting fees help underwrite the Games). Furthermore, the monitoring of athletes who seek illegal competitive advantages, often through the use of performance-enhancing drugs, has been an ongoing challenge. The IOC itself has also been the subject of controversy. In 1998 a scandal erupted with revelations that bribery and favoritism had played a role in the awarding of the 2002 Winter Games to Salt Lake City, Utah, and in the selection of some of the earlier venues. As a result, the IOC instituted a number of reforms including initiating age and term limits for members and barring them from visiting cities bidding to be the Olympic host.

10   Although the evolution of the Olympic Games has led to significant changes, the core purpose and function has remained the same throughout time: peace through competition. With every sporting event and victory lap, our world becomes more of a global community rather than nations being islands in themselves. In this the Olympic Games are a crucial part of our past and our future.

(1,197 words)

Words and Expressions

evolve	/ɪ'vɒlv/	vi.	to develop gradually, or to cause something or someone to develop gradually (使)逐步发展
crucial	/'kruːʃəl/	adj.	extremely important 至关重要的
ultimate	/'ʌltɪmɪt/	adj.	most extreme or important, or final 最终的，首要的
athletic	/æθ'letɪk/	adj.	relating to sports or physical activities 运动的
dominate	/'dɒmɪneɪt/	vt.	to control someone or something or to have more importance than other people or things 控制，支配
accommodate	/ə'kɒmədeɪt/	vt.	to provide with a place to live or to be stored in 容纳
spectator	/spek'teɪtə/	n.	someone who is watching an event or a game 观众，观看者
mythology	/mɪ'θɒlədʒɪ/	n.	set of ancient myths 神话（总称）
sanctuary	/'sæŋktʃuərɪ/	n.	the most holy part of a religious building 圣殿
prestige	/pre'stiːʒ/	n.	the respect and admiration that someone or something attains because of their success, important position in society 威望，声望
initially	/ɪ'nɪʃəlɪ/	adv.	at the beginning of a plan, process, situation, etc. 起初
brag	/bræg/	vt.	to talk too proudly about what you have done, what you own, etc. 自夸，吹嘘
stadion	/'steɪʃən/	n.	the building in which it took place, which became stadium in Latin, and came into the language of English 体育馆
award ceremony			颁奖典礼
call out			大声说出
wreath	/riːθ/	n.	a circular band of leaves placed on someone's head as a sign of victory and honour in ancient Greece 花冠（旧时荣誉的象征）
accomplishment	/ə'kʌmplɪʃmənt/	n.	something successful or impressive that is achieved after a lot of effort and hard work 成绩，成就
eventually	/ɪ'ventʃuəlɪ/	adv.	after a long time, or after a lot of things have happened 最终，终于

Unit 2　Olympics

enforce	/ɪnˈfɔːs/	vt.	to make people obey a rule or law 执行，实施 **enforcement** n. 执行，实施
treaty	/ˈtriːtɪ/	n.	a formal written agreement between two or more countries or governments 条约
pilgrim	/ˈpɪlɡrɪm/	n.	a religious person who travels a long way to a holy place 朝圣者，香客
en route	/ˌɒnˈruːt/	adv.	on the way 在路上，在途中
ensure	/ɪnˈʃʊə/	vt.	to make certain that something will happen properly 保证，确保
proceed	/prəˈsiːd/	vi.	to continue to do something that has already been planned or started 继续进行
thereafter	/ðeərˈɑːftə/	adv.	after a particular event or time 此后，其后
provoke	/prəˈvəʊk/	vt.	to cause a reaction or feeling, especially a sudden one 激起，引起
censure	/ˈsenʃə/	n.	the act of expressing strong disapproval and criticism 声讨，严厉谴责
condemn	/kənˈdem/	vt.	to say very strongly that you do not approve of something or someone, especially because you think it is morally wrong 谴责，责备
pagan	/ˈpeɪɡən/	adj.	relating to or believing in a religion that is not one of the main religions of the world 异教的
spectacle	/ˈspektəkəl/	n.	an unusual or interesting thing or situation that you see or notice—used especially in order to show disapproval（通常贬义）令人注意的目标
revive	/rɪˈvaɪv/	vt.	to bring something back after it has not been used or has not existed for a period of time 复兴
in the face of			面对（问题、困难或危险）
assemble	/əˈsembəl/	vt.	to gather a large number of people or things together in one place or for one purpose 召集，收集
tremendous	/trɪˈmendəs/	adj.	very big, fast, powerful, etc. 巨大的，极快的，强有力的
award	/əˈwɔːd/	vt.	to officially give someone something such as a prize or money to reward them for something they have done 给予，授予
overshadow	/ˌəʊvəˈʃædəʊ/	vt.	to make someone or something else seem less important 使相形见绌
electrical timing			电动计时

onset	/ˈɒnset/	n.	the beginning of something, especially something bad (尤指某种不好事情的)开始，发作
entrant	/ˈentrənt/	n.	someone who takes part in a competition 参赛者，选手
decathlon	/dɪˈkæθlɒn/	n.	an athletic contest comprising 10 different track and field events and won by the contestant having the highest total score 十项全能
heptathlon	/hepˈtæθlən/	n.	a women's sports competition involving seven track and field events 女子七项全能运动
archery	/ˈɑːtʃəri/	n.	the sport of shooting arrows from a bow 射箭（运动）
softball	/ˈsɒftbɔːl/	n.	a game similar to baseball but played on a smaller field with a slightly larger and softer ball 垒球运动
canoe	/kəˈnuː/	n.	a long light boat that is pointed at both ends and which you move along using a paddle 独木舟 **canoeing** n. 划艇运动
kayak	/ˈkaɪæk/	n.	a type of light boat, usually for one person, that is moved using a paddle 皮艇 **kayaking** n. 皮艇运动
equestrian	/ɪˈkwestriən/	adj.	relating to horse-riding 马术的
field hockey			a game played on grass by two teams of 11 players, with sticks and a ball 曲棍球
taekwondo	/taɪˈkwɒndəʊ/	n.	a style of fighting from Korea in which you kick and hit but do not use weapons 跆拳道
modern pentathlon			a sports competition that involves running, swimming, riding horses, fencing, and shooting 现代五项
trampoline	/ˈtræmpəliːn/	n.	a piece of equipment on which you jump up and down as a sport. It consists of a metal frame with a piece of strong cloth stretched tightly over it. 蹦床
triathlon	/traɪˈæθlən/	n.	a sports competition in which competitors run, swim, and cycle long distances 铁人三项（全能）运动
inaugurate	/ɪˈnɔːɡjʊreɪt/	vt.	to start something 开创，开始
ice hockey			a sport played on ice, in which players try to hit a hard flat round object into the other team's goal with special sticks 冰球
curling	/ˈkɜːlɪŋ/	n.	a sport played on ice, in which players slide heavy stones towards a marked place 掷冰壶，冰上溜石
bobsledding	/ˈbɒbsledɪŋ/	n.	a sports event in which people race against each

Unit 2 Olympics

			other in a small vehicle with two long thin metal blades instead of wheels used 雪橇车比赛
luge	/luːʒ/	n.	a vehicle with blades instead of wheels on which you slide down a track made of ice as a sport 短雪橇
skeleton	/ˈskelitən/	n.	a sport in which you slide down a special ice track while lying on your front on a type of sledge, or the vehicle you slide on 俯式冰橇
thwart	/θwɔːt/	vt.	to prevent something from succeeding or prevent someone from doing what they are trying to do 阻挠,阻碍
nationalistic	/ˌnæʃənəˈlɪstɪk/	adj.	having too much pride in one's own country 民族(国家)主义的
fervor	/ˈfɜːvə/	n.	very strong belief or feeling 狂热,极度兴奋
intense	/inˈtens/	adj.	very great in strength or degree 剧烈的,极度的
rivalry	/ˈraɪvəlrɪ/	n.	a situation in which two or more people, teams, or companies are competing for something, especially over a long period of time, and the feeling of competition between them (不断的)竞争
survival	/səˈvaivəl/	n.	the state of continuing to live or exist 继续生存,幸存
assign	/əˈsain/	vt.	to give a particular function or value to 给予,赋予(功能或价值)
feat	/fiːt/	n.	something that is an impressive achievement because it needs a lot of skills, strength, etc. to do 功绩,业绩,壮举
be rooted in sth			源于
mutual	/ˈmjuːtʃuəl/	adj.	(of two or more people or groups) feeling the same emotion, or doing the same thing to or for each other 相互的,彼此的
antagonism	/ænˈtægənɪzəm/	n.	hatred between people or groups of people 敌对,对抗
propaganda	/ˌprɒpəˈgændə/	n.	information which is false or which emphasizes just one part of a situation, used by a government or political group to make people agree with them (政府或政党为了影响民意的虚假或部分虚假的)宣传
Nazi	/ˈnɑːtsɪ/	n.	a member of the National Socialist Party of Adolf Hitler which controlled Germany from 1933 to 1945 纳粹分子

exclusion	/ɪksˈkluːʒən/	n.	being not allowed to take part in something or enter a place 不准参加
kidnap	/ˈkɪdnæp/	vt.	to take someone somewhere illegally by force, often in order to get money for returning them 绑架
terrorist	/ˈterərɪst/	n.	someone who uses violence such as bombing, shooting, etc. to obtain political demands 恐怖分子
license	/ˈlaɪsəns/	vt.	to give official permission for someone to do or produce something, or for an activity to take place 批准, 许可
commercialize	/kəˈmɜːʃəlaɪz/	vt.	to be more concerned with making money from something than about its quality 使……商业化 **commercialization** n. 商业化
underwrite	/ˌʌndəˈraɪt/	vt.	to support an activity, business plan, etc. with money, and to take financial responsibility if it fails 以金钱支持
monitor	/ˈmɒnɪtə/	vt.	to carefully watch and check a situation in order to see how it changes over a period of time 监测, 监视, 监督
performance-enhancing drugs			兴奋剂
ongoing	/ˈɒngəʊɪŋ/	adj.	continuing, or continuing to develop 不断发展中的
controversy	/ˈkɒntrəvɜːsɪ/	n.	a serious argument about something that involves many people and continues for a long time 争论, 争议, 辩论
scandal	/ˈskændl/	n.	an event in which someone important behaves in a bad way that shocks people 丑闻, 丑事
revelation	/ˌrevəˈleɪʃən/	n.	a surprising fact about someone or something that was previously secret and is now made known 被揭露的(惊人)事实
bribery	/ˈbraɪbərɪ/	n.	the act of giving bribes 贿赂, 受贿, 行贿
favoritism	/ˈfeɪvərɪtɪzəm/	n.	treating one person or group better than others in an unfair way 徇私, 偏爱, 偏袒
venue	/ˈvenjuː/	n.	a place where an organized meeting, concert, etc. takes place 举办地点, 举办场所
institute	/ˈɪnstɪtjuːt/	vt.	to introduce or start a system, rule, legal process, etc. 着手, 制定(制度、规则等)
bar	/bɑː/	vt.	to officially prevent someone from entering a place

Unit 2 Olympics

significant	/sigˈnifikənt/ *adj.*	or from doing something 阻止 large enough to be noticeable or have noticeable effects 不可忽略的, 相当数量的

Reading Comprehension

I. **Decide which of the following best states the author's purpose of writing.**

   A. To introduce the origin and history of the Olympic Games.
   B. To stress the purpose and function of the Olympic Games.
   C. To tell the problems and challenges of the Olympic Games.
   D. To emphasize the political influence of the Olympic Games.

II. **Answer the following questions.**

   1. Where and why were the ancient Olympic Games held?
   2. What were the ancient Olympic award ceremonies like?
   3. Who helped revive the modern Olympic Games? What was the purpose of reviving them?
   4. Make a list of some modern Olympic Games and the highlights of those Games.
   5. What is the role of politics in the development of the Olympics? Explain with some examples.
   6. What are some of the policies that the IOC has adopted in order to deal with certain problems?

III. **Judge, according to the text, whether the following statements are true or false. For false statements, write the facts in parentheses.**

   1. Politics have always been important to ensure the peace process and final success of the Games.
      (   )
   2. In ancient times, there were battles fighting for control of the stadium at Olympia because it would bring good luck and considerable fortune.
      (   )
   3. There were neither female nor professional athletes in the ancient Olympics.
      (   )

4. The Olympic Games were eventually discontinued at the end of the fourth century A.D. because of religious factors.
   (   )
5. During the first three modern Olympic Games, there were no gold medals awarded to the winners.
   (   )
6. Women athletes made their debut in the Olympics at the Stockholm Games.
   (   )
7. The Winter Olympic Games are held every four years and in the same year as the Summer Games.
   (   )
8. The IOC is subject to controversy because athletic excellence contributes to rivalries among different nations and countries.
   (   )

IV. Paraphrase, use your own words to explain the sentences in the text with the help of the context.

1. (Para. 1) ... the attempt to gain political advantage through athletic excellence and competition has not changed with the passage of time.

2. (Para. 3) Initially, only amateur male athletes took part in the Games, merely representing their hometowns and earning "bragging rights."

3. (Para. 4) This freed travelers from being pressed into fighting local battles en route to the competition and ensured that the Games would proceed successfully.

4. (Para. 6) Unfortunately, the next two Olympics, held in Paris and St. Louis, were overshadowed by the Paris Universal Exhibition and the Louisiana

Unit 2 Olympics

Purchase Exposition.

5. (Para. 8) As in ancient Greece, nationalistic fervor has fostered intense rivalries that at times have threatened the very survival of the Games.

6. (Para. 8) Between 1952 and 1988 rivalry between the United States and the Soviet Union, rooted in mutual political antagonism, resulted in each boycotting the Games hosted by the other.

7. (Para. 9) As a result, the IOC instituted a number of reforms including initiating age and term limits for members and barring them from visiting cities bidding to be Olympic host.

Vocabulary Exercises

I. **Fill in each blank with one of the two words from each pair and note the difference of meaning between them. Change the form when necessary.**

1. REVIVAL   SURVIVAL
   A. The doctor told my son that I had one-in-ten chance of _____.
   B. The flowers will _____ in water.
   C. Recently, there has been some _____ of ancient music.
   D. There are concerns that few people could _____ the earthquake in the area.

2. CONSIST   CONSTITUTE
   A. The basketball team _____ of four Europeans and two Americans.
   B. Crime and illegal drugs _____ the city's major problems.
   C. The beauty of the plan _____ in its simplicity.
   D. The elderly _____ nearly 25% of the town's population.

3. ENHANCE   ENFORCE
    A. It isn't easy for a new teacher to _____ any sort of discipline.
    B. The publicity has greatly _____ her reputation.
    C. My mother doesn't like to use artificial flavor _____ in her cooking.
    D. The government should strengthen the _____ of laws to prevent alcohol sales to underage persons.
4. ENSURE   CENSURE
    A. The manager was _____ for its lack of decisiveness during the crisis.
    B. The airline is taking steps to _____ safety on its aircrafts.
    C. I have the confidence to _____ that nothing will go wrong tomorrow.
    D. His dishonest behavior came under severe _____ and punishment.

II. Choose a word or phrase that best completes each of the following sentences.

1. The 70-year-old professor sued the university for age _____, because his teaching contract had not been renewed.
    A. possession   B. discrimination   C. commitment   D. employment
2. After the athlete got the gold medal, the audience _____ into wild cheers.
    A. erupted   B. corrupted   C. abrupt   D. bankrupt
3. The UN Secretary-General has _____ both countries to observe the cease-fire.
    A. called by   B. called up   C. called out   D. called on
4. The 1986 Challenger space-shuttle _____ was caused by unusually low temperatures immediately before the launch.
    A. dismay   B. disaster   C. expedition   D. controversy
5. Foreign disinvestment and the _____ of South Africa from world capital markets after 1985 further weakened its economy.
    A. displacement   B. elimination   C. exclusion   D. exception

III. Fill in the blank in each sentence with a word or phrase taken from the box in its appropriate form.

prestige	call out	provoke	condemn	in the face of
inaugurate	boycott	ongoing	thwart	antagonism
bar sb from (doing) sth		initiate	overshadow	

Unit 2 Olympics

1. The custom officers seized his passport and _____ him _____ leaving the country.
2. My cousin was admitted to a highly _____ university.
3. The historic _____ between the two countries resulted in endless wars in this region.
4. The workers were _____ to fix the broken bridge.
5. The swimming pool was closed after being _____ as a health hazard by some experts.
6. Cathy has always felt _____ by her famous sister.
7. My holiday plans have been _____ by Mom's fierce opposition.
8. It is amazing how Daniel has survived _____ strong pressures from his rivals.
9. No evidence has yet been found and the investigations are still _____.
10. An exhibition on Nobel Peace Prize will be _____ here from next Tuesday.
11. His new novel has _____ fierce debate in the literary circles.
12. The union called on its members to _____ all products from that country.
13. In some African tribes, boys are _____ into manhood at the age of thirteen.

Translation Exercises

Translate each of the following sentences into English, using the word or phrase given in the brackets.

1. 国家体育场"鸟巢"是2008年北京奥运会的主体育场,能容纳大约9万名观众。(accommodate)

2. 一支由30余辆豪华轿车组成的车队正围绕市中心巡游,所到之处无不成为市民关注的焦点。(consist of)

3. 他答应借给我们1,500美元,但与我们所需要的款项相比,这点钱实在微不足道。(compare to)

4. 飞机在即将到达伦敦时颠簸了十分钟,而后迫降在附近的机场。(press into)

5. 面对这样的指责,许多人都会选择辞职,然而他却留下来,决心挺过难关。(in the face of)

6. 如果大人总把过错归咎于孩子,而不自我检讨,孩子将逐渐失去自信,变得自闭起来。(assign... to)

7. 国际奥委会禁止运动员、教练员和官员为新闻网站或其他网站撰写第一手的报道。(bar... from)

8. 全体中华儿女都为伟大祖国取得如此辉煌的成就而感到无比骄傲与自豪!(with pride in)

Text II

Barcelona 1992—The Games of the XXVIth Olympiad

Pre-reading Questions

1. What preparations should a city or even the whole country take in order to host a successful Olympic Games?
2. Do you know how the Olympic flame was lit in Barcelona? How was it lit in the 29th Olympic Games in Beijing?

1　　Barcelona, considered one of the Olympic movement's perpetual bridesmaids, tried on four separate occasions to convince the International Olympic Committee (IOC) of its ability to host the Summer Olympics. In 1924, the Spanish city was considered a leading contender for the Games, but Paris received the award, with some help from native son and IOC president Baron Pierre de Coubertin. The city made a bid for the 1936 Olympics and built a stadium on the nearby mountain of Montjuic, only to have the IOC choose Berlin. Barcelona attempted to secure the 1940 Games canceled by World War II, and, finally, a poorly planned effort between Madrid and Barcelona for the 1972 Games ended in failure when Munich was selected as the host city.

Barcelona next pinned its hopes on a bid for the 1992 Games. The organizing committee focused the IOC's attention on the significance of 1992 to Spain: hosting the world during the five hundredth anniversary of Columbus' voyage to the Americas seemed appropriate, and Spain's entry into the European Committee as a full partner deserved a celebration. In addition, the organizing committee prepared a conservative Olympic budget of $667 million, most of which would be secured by television rights and corporate sponsors.

Of the small field of candidates—including Amsterdam, the Netherlands; Brisbane, Australia; Birmingham, England; and Belgrade, Yugoslavia—only Paris and Barcelona were considered likely choices. All of Spain supported Barcelona's bid; 65,000 young Spaniards offered to volunteer if Barcelona won the Games, and ninety-two members of the Catalan business community raised $10 million for the organizing committee's campaign. A promise was made to the IOC that 10 percent of excess revenue from a Barcelona Games would be shared with the IOC and with the Spanish Olympic Committee. The committee's final trump was Juan Antonio Samaranch, president of the IOC and a native of Barcelona. When asked what would happen if Barcelona lost a fifth time, one businessman replied, "Collective suicide." Such drastic steps proved unnecessary; this time the IOC overlooked Paris in favor of Barcelona.

The Olympics served several important functions for Barcelona. After four decades of economic and political oppression under the Franco regime, Barcelona wanted to show its principal rival, Madrid, the European Community, and, indeed, the entire world that the city could host a memorable international event. The Olympics also provided the city with the needed catalyst to overturn decades of neglect by hastening an infrastructure revitalization plan begun in 1980. The city's plan became a reality due to the efforts of one individual who ensured cooperation between the Barcelona Olympic Organizing Committee (COOB) and the city: Pascual Maragall I Mira, mayor of Barcelona and president of COOB. With just six years to work with prior to the Games, Maragall planned to turn Barcelona into a city that would serve the Olympic family and provide residents with a comfortable urban environment well into the twenty-first century.

5   In what art critic Robert Hughes described as "the most ambitious project of its kind that any government of a 20th-century city has tried," Barcelona began its preparations for the Olympic spotlight with a massive construction campaign for venues and urban improvements. To curb costs, COOB took great care in choosing existing buildings that could serve as venues and in commissioning innovative architects to enhance the city's design-conscious reputation. New facilities built on Montjuic truly made the mountain the crown jewel of the city.

6   Living up to the ideal that all residents should benefit from the Games, infrastructure activity encompassed more than Olympic housing and venues. In addition to new facilities on Montjuic, Olympic planners methodically targeted venues for neighborhoods with little or no access to sports facilities.

7   With the concerns of nations addressed, Barcelona was ready to welcome the world. The opening ceremonies dazzled millions of television viewers. Without doubt, the most memorable event of the evening occurred with the lighting of the Olympic flame. Disabled archer Antonio Rebollo shot a flaming arrow 230 feet from the floor of the stadium to the titanium dish above to light the Olympic flame, thus opening the largest Games in the history of the Olympic movement. The 1992 Summer Olympics fielded 9,959 athletes from 172 countries, all of whom received free accommodations during their competitions, another Olympic first. The Games expanded to twenty-six events with the addition of badminton and baseball as medal sports, while pelota, taekwondo, and roller hockey became the last demonstration sports allowed in the Olympics. The Games also opened wider doors to professionalism as professional sailors and basketball players competed for the first time.

8   During the sixteen days, the Games created legends and produced spectacular stories. Even when world records remained intact, the Olympics generated memorable moments. Yet the Barcelona Games were not without controversy as drugs continued to plague the Olympics, with five athletes expelled for use of performance-enhancing substances.

9   In spite of the more infamous moments of the 1992 Games, Barcelona produced one of the more memorable Olympics since World War II. There was no organized boycott, and athletes from sixty-four participating nations won medals, another record. Yet the cost for planning such an occasion was high. Taxes rose faster than inflation for the five years preceding the Games.

10   The city accomplished in six years what would otherwise have taken fifty to accomplish. The longstanding improvements to the city cannot be overlooked, nor can the organizers' success in hosting a successful Olympic Games.

(898 words)

Reading Comprehension

I. Answer the following questions with the information you got from the passage.
1. When did Barcelona first bid for the Olympics? How many bids did it make before it was successful?
2. Why did Barcelona pin its hopes on a bid for the 1992 Games?
3. What was the ideal in the Barcelona Games construction?
4. Why did Robert Hughes describe it as "the most ambitious project of its kind that any government of a 20th-century city has tried"?
5. Why does the author say that Barcelona produced one of the more memorable Olympics since World War II?

Exercises for Integrated Skills

I. Dictation

Listen to the following passage. Altogether the passage will be read to you four times. During the first reading, which will be read at normal speed, listen and try to understand the meaning. For the second and third readings, the passage will be read sentence by sentence, or phrase by phrase, with intervals of 15 to 20 seconds. The last reading will be done at normal speed again and during this time you should check your work. You will then be given 2 minutes to check through your work once more.

II. Cloze

Fill in each blank in the passage below with the help of the initial letter given.

Olympic Games, international sports competition, are held every four years at a different site, in which athletes from different nations compete against each other in a v___1___ of sports. There are two t___2___ of Olympics, the Summer Olympics and the Winter Olympics. Through 1992 they were held in the same year, but beginning in 1994 they were r___3___ so that they are held in alternate even-numbered years. For example, the Winter Olympics were held in 1994 and the Summer Olympics in 1996. The Winter Olympics were next held in 1998, and the Summer Olympics next o___4___ in 2000.

The Winter Olympic Games were first held as a s___5___ competition in 1924 at Chamonix-Mont-Blanc（查默尼克斯，全名为查默尼克斯勃朗峰，法国小镇，滑雪胜地）, France. From that time until 1992, they took place the same year as the Summer Games. However, beginning with the 1994 Winter Olympics in Lillehammer（利勒哈默尔，挪威奥普兰郡首府）, Norway, the Winter Games were rescheduled to occur in the middle of the Olympic c___6___, alternating on e___7___ years with the Summer Games. The 1924 Winter Games included 14 events in five different sports. By c___8___, the program for the 2002 Winter Games, held in Salt Lake City, Utah, included more than 75 events in 15 different sports.

Oral Activities

Activity One

The Olympic Creed reads, "The most important thing in the Olympic Games is not to win but to take part, just as the most important thing in life is not the triumph but the struggle. The essential thing is not to have conquered but to have fought well." Do you agree with this statement? Why or why not? Use examples to support your opinion.

Activity Two

The Chinese people have successfully hosted the 29th Olympiad, leaving a valuable and positive legacy for China. Discuss with your partner what the legacy

Unit 2　Olympics

is. Your discussion can include the sporting venues, the environmental improvements, the infrastructure, and/or the people's manners.

Writing Practice

Note Writing: Offering Note

You have two tickets for a CBA match for this coming Sunday. Your friend Kevin is a keen basketball fan. Write him a note to offer the opportunity for him to go with you to watch the game. You should write in about 60 words.

September _____

Kevin,

David

Passage Writing:

After hearing that Beijing won the bid to host the 2008 Olympic Games, what was your feeling? During the 2008 Olympic Games, what were the memorable moments in your heart? Write a short passage of around 200 words expressing your own feelings about the 2008 Olympics. Your experiences in the Olympic Games (i.e. watching them, visiting the venues, etc.) can also be included in the passage.

Unit 3 Education

Warm-up Activities

1. What realistic changes would you like to make to our traditional attitudes toward education?
2. What are some of the simulations of real life practiced in college? What are some essential life skills you develop on your own? What do you think is more important?

Text I

Lifelong Learning

Pre-reading Questions

1. Do you think that lifelong learning is a must? Why or why not?
2. What are your attitudes toward distance learning?

1 We all learn in one way or another throughout our lives and, with the strides which have been made in recent years in medicine and technology, people can expect to live longer, healthier lives than ever before. Although education has traditionally focused on the needs of young people, increasingly, there is a large population of older people who are still active in body and mind and who want to expand their intellectual horizons in ways which, perhaps because of family, vocational or financial reasons, may not have been possible for them previously. Other people are unable to take advantage of traditional learning situations because of disabilities of one kind or another, or because other circumstances of their lives, such as geographical location, make it difficult, if not impossible, for

them to attend regular classes. In order to meet this growing demand, many universities are setting up programs to cater for the needs of a wide range of people in a variety of circumstances.

2   The Open University, for instance, has operated in the United Kingdom for a number of years. Open University students work within a small group who communicate with their tutor and with each other by post, fax or telephone and, in more recent years, by email. The tutor marks the students' work, comments upon it, offers any assistance required and generally monitors the students' progress. Students usually have an opportunity to attend a number of day schools, which bring the group together for group tutoring at particular stages of the course. Learning materials consist of textbooks, assignment sheets, and computer software, as well as audio or video materials. The Open University also works in collaboration with the British Broadcasting Corporation (BBC) to broadcast programs related to the courses. Increasingly, computers have become an intrinsic part of many Open University studies which stress the importance of acquiring computer skills, many of which will be valuable after the completion of the course.

3   The Virtual University, which operates in Canada, is another example of an educational institution which specializes in distance learning. It has no campus, no faculty buildings, no sports facilities. However, it has a curriculum which includes several thousand courses and several hundred degrees, diplomas and certificates at a number of universities across Canada. Virtual University students report appreciating the flexibility they can achieve by means of this kind of education: instead of being tied to fixed lecture times and locations, they can study where and when it is convenient for their own individual circumstances.

4   In previous times, a typical classroom used to be a place where teachers and students worked together to explore a wonderful world of knowledge. Distance learning used to be considered the poor relation of education, used only by those for whom attending classes was physically impossible because, perhaps, they lived on remote rural farms or in remote fishing villages. But now modern technology has taken over those interactions and introduced us to a

whole new approach to learning. Distance learning by Internet is no longer undertaken only by those who are geographically remote: for many students it is a viable option which they choose irrespective of their physical location.

5   Many people believe that learning via the Internet is more successful than conventional forms of education. It is more flexible and it is accessible anywhere, anytime. It saves time and money and it is extremely convenient. Instead of having to go to a library or university centre, a library is available in students' homes 24 hours a day, seven days a week, and it never closes for holidays. They can connect to the materials they need, check with their supervisors and exchange insights with their classmates without leaving the comfort and convenience of their own homes. There is no time limitation so that students can repeat exercises as many times as they need, whenever it is convenient for them. And they don't have to waste hours and a lot of money traveling to and from lectures. The time that is saved can be put to much better use studying and completing assignments. In these ways, distance education can be adapted to suit the needs of individual students and allowances can be made for individual circumstances such as family and employment commitments.

6   From an administrative point of view, Internet learning has a number of advantages. Traditional educational institutions require land and buildings, which are expensive, and teachers' wages are continuously increasing. Furthermore, traditional courses usually depend on books and other paper-based materials which are much more costly than electronic materials. Internet classes and courses are also very convenient because there are no physical restrictions such as space, time and transport limitations as in conventional education. In classroom-based courses, there is a limitation to the number of students who can physically fit into a particular space, whereas this is not an issue for Internet education which is therefore available to anyone who is interested.

7   Margaret Steele is an example of a student who did not plan to take distance education courses. She was married with two children and had a part-time job as an accountant. But in her late twenties she found her speech becoming slurred, and she became increasingly unsteady on her feet. After a number of medical tests were carried out, she was diagnosed as suffering from Multiple Sclerosis, a serious neurological disease which left her unable to walk and dependent on a wheelchair to get around.

Unit 3 Education

8   "This was an extremely traumatic time for me and the family", says Margaret. "I had always taken my health for granted, but suddenly I was the victim of a cruel disease and there was nothing I could do about it. It would have been very easy to give up and spend the rest of my life feeling sorry for myself, but I decided to have a look at the options that were available to me."

9   Since she was unable to continue with her previous job, Margaret decided to extend her education and take a distance education course. It is hard work, but, according to Margaret, it is worth it for the children's sake as well as for her own satisfaction. She feels she sets a good example for the children, and she will be better able to help them as they pursue their own education. The opportunity to engage in distance education means that her disability does not totally dominate her life. Also, the extra qualifications she has so far gained have enabled her to set up a small accounting practice of her own at home, so she now has increased financial independence.

10   Margaret is a successful student, who has so far passed all her courses. She plans to complete her bachelor's degree then continue on to obtain an online master's degree, maybe even a doctorate. After graduation, she hopes to work with injured or disabled individuals, possibly in a counseling or a rehabilitation role. Her teachers consider her an outstanding student and an inspiration to others, and they are convinced that with her indomitable spirit she will achieve her goal.

11   Distance education, then, is a way for people to continue with their education irrespective of their geographical location or the circumstances of their lives. In order to succeed at this kind of course, students need to be motivated and capable of employing time management and self-control strategies which ensure that work is completed in spite of the absence of obvious external discipline in the form of a lecturer or tutor. It is very easy to let time slip by and for deadlines to pass with work unfinished. Although many students respond positively to this kind of study, others find it is too lonely: they need the interaction with others to motivate them and help keep them going through the long and sometimes boring hours which are required to successfully complete this kind of course. However, for those who possess the necessary qualities and skills, aided by modern technology, lifelong learning is now an achievable goal for everyone, limited only by the individual's will to succeed.

(1,341 words)

Words and Expressions

stride	/straɪd/	n.	an improvement in a situation or in the development of something 进展，进步
horizon	/həˈraɪzən/	n.	the limit of your ideas, knowledge, and experience 知识（思想、经验等的）最大范围；眼界，见识
cater for			to provide a particular group of people with the things they need or want 迎合，投合
monitor	/ˈmɒnɪtə/	vt.	to carefully watch and check a situation in order to see how it changes over a period of time 监视，监控
collaboration	/kəˌlæbəˈreɪʃən/	n.	the act of working together with another person or group to achieve something, especially in science or art 合作，协作
intrinsic	/ɪnˈtrɪnsɪk/	adj.	being part of the nature or character of someone or something 内在的，固有的，本质的
completion	/kəmˈpliːʃən/	n.	the act of finishing something 完成，结束
faculty	/ˈfækəltɪ/	n.	all the teachers in a university 全体教员
flexibility	/ˌfleksɪˈbɪlɪtɪ/	n.	the ability to change or be changed easily to suit a different situation 机动性，灵活性 **flexible** adj. 灵活的
viable	/ˈvaɪəbəl/	adj.	capable of doing what it is intended to do 可行的
irrespective of sth			regardless of something; without being affected or influenced by something 不考虑，不顾
via	/ˈvaɪə/	prep.	using a particular person, machine, etc. to send something 通过
accessible	/əkˈsesɪbəl/	adj.	easy to obtain or use 易得到的，可用的
allowance	/əˈlaʊəns/	n.	something you take into account in your decisions, plans, or actions 考虑
slur	/slɜː/	vt.	to speak unclearly without separating your words or sounds correctly 含糊地发(音)
diagnose	/ˈdaɪəgnəʊz/	vt.	to find out what illness someone has, or what the cause of a fault is, after doing tests, examinations, etc. 诊断(疾病)
neurological	/ˌnjʊərəʊˈlɒdʒɪkəl/	adj.	related to the nervous system 神经学的，神经病学的
traumatic	/trɔːˈmætɪk/	adj.	shocking and upsetting, psychologically damaging 痛苦而难忘的

rehabilitate	/ˌriːhəˈbɪlɪteɪt/	vt.	to help someone live a normal life again after they have had a serious illness or been in prison 使康复;使(改造罪犯)恢复正常生活 **rehabilitation** *n.* 恢复,复原
convince	/kənˈvɪns/	vt.	to make someone feel certain that something is true 使确信,使信服
indomitable	/ɪnˈdɒmɪtəbəl/	adj.	having great determination or courage 不可屈服的,不屈不挠的,不气馁的

Reading Comprehension

I. Decide which of the following best states the author's purpose for writing.

   A. To stress the importance of lifelong learning.

   B. To inform the reader that distance education is inescapable in the future.

   C. To tell the reader that lifelong learning is made possible by distance education, limited only by the individual's willpower.

II. Answer the following questions.

   1. What is so special about the Virtual University in Canada?

   2. What characteristics are typical of the traditional classroom?

   3. What advantages does online learning have?

   4. Why does the author give us an example of Margaret Steele?

   5. According to the author, what is the future of lifelong learning?

III. Choose the best answers to the following questions with the information from the passage.

   1. Which of the following statements about traditional education is a restriction?

      A. Young people as the majority.

      B. Fixed lecture times.

      C. Fixed locations.

      D. All of the above.

   2. Which of the following is not part of a tutor's job in an Open University?

      A. Grading.

      B. Lecturing.

C. Monitoring.

D. Offering help.

3. Distance education is more successful than conventional education because _____.

   A. distance learning is more flexible

   B. distance learning is accessible anywhere, anytime

   C. distance learning helps save money and time

   D. all of the above

4. Margaret Steele didn't think of taking distance education courses because _____.

   A. she had a suitable education for her previous part-time job

   B. taking distance education courses was a lot of work

   C. she was satisfied with her previous education

   D. there was nothing she particularly wanted to learn

5. Margaret's life was changed by a serious neurological disease so that she _____.

   A. needed constant help in her daily life

   B. couldn't live without her doctor's help

   C. needed to use a wheelchair

   D. had to hire a person to take care of her

6. Distance education was of great importance to Margaret because _____.

   A. she could become a better educated person

   B. she could set a good example for her children and help them

   C. she could have other opportunities to work and achieve her goals

   D. all of the above

7. Which of the following is NOT a necessary quality for students who choose distance education?

   A. They need to be able to manage their own time.

   B. They need to be active in communication with others.

   C. They need to know how to control themselves.

   D. They need to be self-motivated.

Unit 3 Education

IV. **Paraphrase, use your own words to explain the sentences in the text with the help of the context.**

1. (Para. 1) Although education has traditionally focused on the needs of young people, increasingly, there is a large population of older people who are still active in body and mind and who want to expand their intellectual horizons in ways which, perhaps because of family, vocational or financial reasons, may not have been possible for them previously.

   _____

   _____

2. (Para. 2) Increasingly, computers have become an intrinsic part of many Open University studies which stress the importance of acquiring computer skills, many of which will be valuable after the completion of the course.

   _____

   _____

3. (Para. 3) Virtual University students report appreciating the flexibility they can achieve by means of this kind of education: instead of being tied to fixed lecture times and locations they can study as, where and when it is convenient for their own individual circumstances.

   _____

   _____

4. (Para. 4) Distance learning by Internet is no longer undertaken only by those who are geographically remote: for many students it is a viable option which they choose irrespective of their physical location.

   _____

   _____

5. (Para. 5) In these ways, distance education can be adapted to suit the needs of individual students and allowances can be made for individual circumstances such as family and employment commitments.

   _____

   _____

6. (Para. 11) In order to succeed at this kind of course, students need to be motivated and capable of employing time management and self-control strategies which ensure that work is completed in spite of the absence of obvious exter-

nal discipline in the form of a lecturer or tutor.

Vocabulary Exercises

I. **Fill in each blank with one of the two words from each pair and note the difference of meaning between them. Change the form when necessary.**

   1. FACILITY   EQUIPMENT
      A. This is a 5-star hotel with fantastic _____.
      B. Helen has an amazing _____ for mental arithmetic.
   2. LIMIT   LIMITATION
      A. There is always a _____ to the amount of time when we are taking exams.
      B. As the old saying goes, a wise man knows his own _____.
      C. Deafness is a serious _____ in this job.
      D. The speed _____ is the fastest speed you are allowed to drive a car at.
   3. CONVENTIONAL   TRADITONAL
      A. My grandmother's opinions are rather narrow and _____.
      B. More and more foreign people are interested in _____ Chinese medicine.
      C. It is _____ for the bride to make a speech in the wedding ceremony.

II. **Choose a word or phrase that best completes each of the following sentences.**

   1. It's a good move _____ in his career.
      A. at this stage   B. on the stage   C. in stages   D. for the stage
   2. The dinner _____ several different Korean dishes.
      A. consisted in   B. consisted of   C. composed of   D. made up of
   3. We need someone _____ bright new ideas.
      A. of   B. on   C. by   D. with
   4. They own a house in France _____ a villa in Spain.
      A. except   B. with   C. as well as   D. in addition

Unit 3　Education

5. There have been a lot of changes _____ the department since I came.
   A. to   B. from   C. within   D. with

III. **Fill in the blank in each sentence with a word or phrase taken from the box in its appropriate form.**

intrinsic	dominate	cater for	take over
irrespective	collaboration	rehabilitation	indomitable
consist	take advantage of		

1. In spring, we usually set the clock ahead one hour, to _____ the summer daylight.
2. Our politicians should learn to _____ the man in the street.
3. An American company _____ with a Swiss firm to develop the product.
4. English is an _____ part of the school curriculum.
5. Peter will _____ as managing director when Bill retires.
6. The household may now _____ of several teenagers or an elderly relative.
7. The law applies to everyone _____ of race, religion or color.
8. Men still tend to _____ the world of law—hardly any top judges are women.
9. The prison service should try to _____ prisoners so that they can lead normal lives when they leave prison.
10. This _____ spirit contributes to the victory for world peace and justice.

Translation Exercises

Translate each of the following sentences into English, using the word or phrase given in the brackets.

1. 大学毕业后, 他就把所有的精力都放在工作上。(focus on)

2. 有些生产商为了推广他们的产品利用广告来欺骗消费者。
   (take advantage of)

3. 为了满足读者对科学知识的不断需求,国家图书馆计划订阅更多的科技杂志。(cater for)

4. 这家印度餐馆提供的自助餐不仅包括各种各样具有印度风味的特色菜,还有常见的甜点、海鲜和饮料。(consist of)

5. 为了顺利完成这次调查任务,我们必须加强与当地政府和人民的联系与合作。(in collaboration with)

6. 此次农村医疗改革使得广大农民都有权享受优质的医疗服务。(accessible)

7. 刚入校的新生发现自己很难适应这里的气候与学习环境。(adapt to)

8. 他满以为自己能通过考试,结果还是以失败而告终。(take... for granted)

9. 尽管病重,他仍然积极忙于慈善学校的教学,我们都佩服他那不屈不饶的精神。(engage in/ indomitable)

Text II

Angels on a Pin

Pre-reading Questions

What are the traditional teaching and testing methods in China? Try to comment on these methods.

1 Some time ago, I received a call from Jim, a colleague of mine, who teaches physics. He asked me if I would do him a favor and be the referee on the grading of an examination question. I said sure, but I did not quite understand why he should need my help. He told me that he was about to give a student a

zero for his answer to a physics question, but the student protested that it wasn't fair. He insisted that he deserved a perfect score if the system were not set up against the student. Finally, they agreed to take the matter to an impartial instructor. And I was selected.

I went to my colleague's office and read the examination question. It said: "Show how it is possible to determine the height of a tall building with the aid of a barometer." The student has answered: "Take the barometer to the top of the building, tie a long rope to it, lower the barometer to the street, and then bring it up and measure the length of the rope. The length of the rope will be the height of the building."

I laughed and pointed out to my colleague that we must admit the student really had a pretty strong case for full credit since he had indeed answered the question completely and correctly. On the other hand, I could also see the dilemma because if full credit were given to him it could mean a high grade for the student in his physics course. A high grade is supposed to prove competence in the course, but the answer he gave did not show his knowledge on the subject. "So, what would you do if you were me?" Jim asked. I suggested that the student have another try at answering the question. I was not surprised that my colleague agreed, but I was surprised that the student did, too.

I told the student that I would give him six minutes to answer the question. But I warned him that this time his answer should show some knowledge of physics. He sat down and picked up his pen. He appeared to be thinking hard. At the end of five minutes, however, I noticed that he had not put down a single word. I asked him if he wished to give up, but he said no. He had not written anything down because he had too many possible answers to this problem. He was just trying to decide which would be the best one. I excused myself for interrupting him and asked him to go on. In the next minute, he dashed off his answer, which read: "Take the barometer to the top of the building and lean over the edge of the roof. Drop the barometer and time its fall with a stopwatch. Then, using the formula $S=1/2\ at^2$, calculate the height of the building."

At this point, I asked my colleague if he would give up. He nodded yes, and I gave the student almost full credit.

When I left my colleague's office, I recalled that the student had said that he had other answers to the problem. I was curious, so I asked him what they were. "Oh, yes," said the student. "There are many ways of getting the height of a tall building with the aid of a barometer. For example, you could take the barometer out in a sunny day and measure the height of the barometer, the length of its shadow, and the length of the shadow of the building, and by the use of a simple proportion, determine the height of the building. The beauty of this method is that you don't have to drop the barometer and break it."

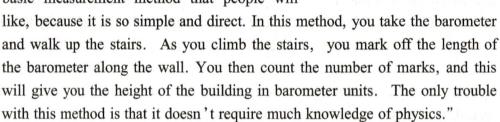

7 "Fine," I said. "Any more?"

8 "Yes," said the student. "There is a very basic measurement method that people will like, because it is so simple and direct. In this method, you take the barometer and walk up the stairs. As you climb the stairs, you mark off the length of the barometer along the wall. You then count the number of marks, and this will give you the height of the building in barometer units. The only trouble with this method is that it doesn't require much knowledge of physics."

9 "Of course, if you prefer a more sophisticated method, a method that will really show some knowledge of physics, you can tie the barometer to the end of a rope, swing it as a pendulum and determine the value of 'g' at the street level and at the top of the building. From the difference between the two values of 'g' the height of the building can, in principle, be worked out."

10 Finally, he concluded that while there are many ways of solving the problem, "Probably the best and the most practical in a real-life situation is to take the barometer to the basement and knock on the superintendent's door. When the superintendent answers, you speak to him as follows: Mr. Superintendent, I have here a fine barometer. If you will tell me the height of this building, I will gladly give you this barometer!"

11 At this point, I asked the student if he really didn't know the expected answer to this question. He smiled and admitted that he did, but said he was fed up with standard answers to standard questions. He couldn't understand why there should be so much emphasis on fixed rules rather than creative thinking. So he could not resist the temptation to play a little joke with the educational

system, which had been thrown into such a panic by the successful launching of the Russian Sputnik.

12   At that moment I suddenly remembered the question: How many angels can dance on the head of a pin? We teachers are always blaming the students for giving wrong answers. Perhaps we should ask ourselves whether we are always asking the right questions.

(1,197 words)

Reading Comprehension

I. **Answer the following questions with the information you got from the passage.**
   1. What did the author think when five minutes passed and the student had not put down a single word? Why did it take the student so long? Did the student find the question difficult to answer?
   2. What was the answer the student gave finally? Use your own words to tell your classmates.
   3. How did the author score the student? Did Jim consider it fair?
   4. What was really the best way of determining the height of the building? Why?

II. **Topics for discussion and reflection.**
   1. What kind of student is depicted in this story? Use your imagination and give a description of him. Give your opinion about the two professors in the text. Have you ever had teachers like them?
   2. What do you think of the educational system in general and the examination system in particular? Do you agree with this student that there is something terribly wrong with the way the system works?

Exercises for Integrated Skills

I. **Dictation**

   Listen to the following passage. Altogether the passage will be read to you four times. During the first reading, which will be read at normal speed, listen and try to understand the meaning. For the second and third readings, the passage will be read sentence by sentence, or phrase by phrase, with intervals

of 15 to 20 seconds. The last reading will be done at normal speed again and during this time you should check your work. You will then be given 2 minutes to check through your work once more.

_____
_____
_____

II. **Cloze**

Fill in each blank in the passage below with a word taken from the box in its appropriate form.

ask	deadline	emphasize	consistent	clean
practise	master	score	watch	organize
continual	miss	priority		

The kids at the top of the class get there by ___1___ a few basic techniques that others can learn. Here are the secrets of Straight-A students.

1. Set ___2___. Once the books are open or the computer is booted up, phone calls will not be answered, or TV shows ___3___.

2. Some work late at night when the house is quiet. Others wake early. Still others study as soon as they come home from school. All agree, however, on the need for ___4___.

3. Get ___5___. Don't waste time looking for a pencil or ___6___ paper. Keep everything right where you can put your hands on it.

4. Learn how to read. The secret of good reading is to be an active reader— ___7___ asking questions leads to a full understanding of the author's message.

5. Plan your time. If you want A's, you make sure to finish all tasks before the ___8___.

6. Take good notes and use them. The teacher is going to test you on what he or she ___9___. That's what you find in your notes.

7. ___10___ up your act. Clean papers are likely to get higher grades than dirty ones.

8. Test yourself. Students who make up possible test questions often find many

Unit 3 Education

of the same questions on the real exam and then ___11___ higher.
9. Do more than you ___12___. Part of learning is ___13___. The more you practise, the more you learn.

Oral Activities

Activity One
Group discussion: How do you understand education?

Look at the following quotations and share your opinions about education.

"Education is not the filling of a pail, but the lighting of a fire."(William Butler Yeats)

"Education is a producer of wealth, in a large sense, which leads to prosperity, which in turn leads to a high civilization."(Dr. John A. Widstoe)

"If a man empties his purse into his head, no man can take it away from him. An investment in knowledge always pays the best interest."(Benjamin Franklin)

"Education is the ability to listen to almost anything without losing your temper or your self-confidence."(Robert Frost)

"The illiterate of the 21st century will not be those who cannot read and write, but those who cannot learn, unlearn, and relearn." (Alvin Toffler)

Activity Two
Debate: Will five-star preschool education really give kids an edge?

With a strong belief that "the more you invest now, the more you get repaid in the future", parents attach more and more importance to early childhood education. As a result, there is a growing number of high-priced kindergartens with modern, first-class facilities and high-end programs. What do you think of this trend in education? Will five-star preschool education really give kids an edge?

Writing Practice

Note Writing: Introduction Note

Mary, your old classmate, is going to stay with you for several days in your apartment. You are going to be out when she arrives. Leave a note to Sophia, your roommate, to introduce Mary and ask her to take care of Mary. You should write in about 60 words.

> September _____
>
> Sophia,
>
>
>
>
>
> Tina

Passage Writing:

Lifelong learning is the current social development trend, and distance learning has been made possible by advances in Internet and telecommunication technology. How do you like distance learning? Is it really better than traditional learning? Write a short passage of around 200 words stating your own opinion.

Unit 4 Manners

Warm-up Activities

1. Why are manners important? What advice would you give a foreigner visiting your country about how to show good manners?
2. Brainstorm a list of table manners, and then gather in small groups to act out a dinner table scene about things people should or should not do at the dinner table.

Text I

Mind Your Manners

Pre-reading Questions

1. When you were a child, how did your parents teach you manners?
2. How can you help a child develop good manners?

1   In a world full of obstacles, that is sometimes tumultuous, the concept of treating other human beings with kindness and of meeting social expectations is still among the basic skills parents are expected to teach their children. This concept, for children, translates into learning a myriad of manners, which represent behavior appropriate for the society in which they operate. From generation to generation parents strive to teach their children "good manners", which represent society's expectations regarding how they should act. Parents do this in order to make life easier for their children to navigate and to smooth the inevitable points of interaction with others. The instruction "mind your manners" is commonly heard as parents strive to teach their children to behave in a socially ac-

ceptable fashion.

2   Manners can be broken down into two different types: socially acceptable actions and respectful behavior towards others. Socially acceptable actions, or etiquette, are manners that differ in each society. In America, children are taught manners such as saying "yes sir", "no sir", "thank you", "no thanks" and many other phrases to show politeness. Saying these phrases often leaves a good impression on those involved. Table manners and phone etiquette are also some of the most important manners children are taught and most experts feel that it is never too early to start teaching children manners. Children are taught these standards of etiquette from a very early age, and it is an extremely daunting task for most parents.

3   Fortunately, children tend automatically to please the adults around them. To receive praise and rewards is a fundamental need for children. Most parents recognize this need and begin planting the seed of etiquette early. As children like to mimic behavior, parents must model the etiquette they wish to see their children perform. For example, if a society's expectation of a person is that they say "please" and "thank you" before a request is granted, parents must continuously say these phrases in every situation to show their children the effects of good etiquette. By setting a good example, parents are demonstrating to their children that if they say these phrases they will, more than likely, get what they want as a result of showing politeness. Parents must consistently model what they expect from their children. Unfortunately, children are extremely perceptive and have a keen sense of what is heart-felt and what is merely a performance. So, if parents are rude or are not genuine in their politeness, children will sense this and reflect the same behavior and attitudes. In the long run, this will result in a much more difficult social experience for children in their adult years.

4   What if children are not taught basic etiquette? Since etiquette exists to satisfy and achieve social acceptance, a child lacking these skills will grow up to be socially clumsy and ostracised. Often these children have difficulty in school,

are unable to make friends and feel outcast from a very early age. The perception that other members of a society seem to easily achieve their goals and be accepted by others because they have been taught what society expects of them can often breed frustration as a child matures into an adult. This situation, in extreme but not rare cases, even leads to violent behavior owing to the lack of knowledge about social expectations.

5 "Treat others as you want to be treated" is a difficult concept for parents to teach their little ones. This aspect of manners is not instinctual to children. Children pass through many stages from birth to adulthood, and during these stages, parents are saddled with the enormous task of redirecting their children's selfish, self-gratifying actions into those of thoughtful, respectful little human beings. At one year old, most children do not want to play with other children and resist sharing their toys because they are in a stage where they believe the world revolves around them and only them. This is the point when parents often become very self conscientious for their children because they know that society will not tolerate this type of behavior in the very near future. Some parents start to force their children to do what is not within their nature or even within their ability at this time. Instead of modeling the behavior they wish to see in their children they find themselves trying to push them to move through all the developmental stages at a rapid pace.

6 However, training children to behave in a respectful manner goes beyond merely telling a child what to do or what to say. Behavior displaying respect is developed through a consciousness of others and their feelings. Only once children realize that others possess emotions and are able to foresee the consequence of their actions will an authentic attitude of respect develop. When children do not see genuine displays of respect or are not given direction by their parents in the methods of controlling their basic urges, they are likely to develop into self-centered adults who are emotionally incapable of caring for others or managing their own lives in harmony with others.

7 Although details of etiquette are based in cultural values, the need for standards of appropriate behavior is cross-cultural. This is because of the universal human need for an organized, predictable environment. The main difference from one culture to another is the method of instilling these values and the exact nature of the behavior expected.

8   In America, parents are responsible for being the main source of guidance for their children; thus, parents have a round-the-clock job of teaching their children what to do and what not to do. This also means that if children fail to perform to society's expectations at any point in their lives, the parents will bear that burden of responsibility and blame. By contrast, in many cultures around the world, children are viewed and treated as belonging to a community, and everybody is responsible for their upbringing. If children misbehave in public, whether accompanied by their parents or alone, it is a typical practice for an adult to correct them and even reprimand them on the spot in a way which would cause offence in America. Thus the entire society participates in the molding of the young person's character. This can only work if each person holds the same strong values; this method of discipline and guidance is unlikely to work in the American culture where independence and intense individuality are the norm.

9   As the world is evolving into a global community and cultural lines are being blurred, parents must prepare their children to respect others through tolerant and accepting behavior wherever they may be. In today's world, children have a unique opportunity to know and experience many different cultures and they have a chance to share their values with others. The most important job for adults today is to ensure that all children understand the values of their society and are capable of showing respect to others in a way that promotes peace and understanding. It is far too common that the basic attitude of tolerance and respect is set aside or abandoned, and the result is chaos or even blood-shed. As elementary or insignificant it might seem at the time, teaching manners to children is actually a lifelong gift enabling them to positively bring about long-term changes in their world.

(1,229 words)

Words and Expressions

obstacle /ˈɒbstəkəl/   n.   something that makes it difficult for you to go somewhere or to succeed at something 障碍，妨碍

tumultuous /tjuːˈmʌltʃuəs/   adj.   full of noise and excitement 吵闹的，喧哗的

Unit 4 Manners

a myriad of			a very large number of 很多的，无数的
strive	/straɪv/	vi.	to make a great effort to achieve something 努力，奋斗
navigate	/ˈnævɪgeɪt/	vt.	to understand or deal with something complicated 理解，处理（复杂的事情）
smooth	/smuːð/	vt.	to make free from roughness or difficulty 使……顺利
etiquette	/ˈetɪket/	n.	the formal rules for polite behaviour in society or in a particular group 礼节，礼仪
daunting	/ˈdɔːntɪŋ/	adj.	frightening in a way that makes you feel less confident 令人胆怯的，使人气馁的
mimic	/ˈmɪmɪk/	vt.	to copy the way someone talks and behaves, usually to make people laugh 模仿
perceptive	/pəˈseptɪv/	adj.	quick to notice or understand things 有悟性的，有理解力的
clumsy	/ˈklʌmzɪ/	adj.	tactless, unskillful 不圆滑的，缺乏技巧的
ostracise	/ˈɒstrəsaɪz/	vt.	to refuse to accept someone as a member of the group with an unfriendly way deliberately 排斥 **ostracised** adj. 被排除在外的，遭排斥的
outcast	/ˈaʊtkɑːst/	adj.	not accepted by society 被遗弃的，无家可归的
instinctual	/ɪnˈstɪŋktʃʊəl/	adj.	behaving or reacting naturally and without thinking 本能的，直觉的
saddle sb with sth			to make someone responsible for a difficult or boring job (or problem) that they do not want 使负重责，加重担于某人
conscientious	/ˌkɒnʃɪˈenʃəs/	adj.	careful to do everything that it is your job or duty to do 有责任心的，尽责的
predictable	/prɪˈdɪktəbəl/	adj.	happening or behaving in a way that you expect and not unusual or interesting 可预测的，可预示的
instill	/ɪnˈstɪl/	vt.	to teach someone to think, behave, or feel in a particular way over a period of time 逐渐灌输（思想等）
reprimand	/ˈreprɪmɑːnd/	vt.	to tell someone officially that something they have done is very wrong 谴责，申斥
blurred	/blɜːd/	adj.	not clear 模糊不清的
abandon	/əˈbændən/	vt.	to leave someone, especially someone you are responsible for 抛弃，遗弃
chaos	/ˈkeɪɒs/	n.	a situation where there is no order at all and everyone is confused 混乱，纷乱

Reading Comprehension

I. How much did you understand the passage on the first reading? Write down in your own words one or two sentences about the passage.

II. Write down the sentence or the key words that best sum up the main idea in each paragraph.

Para. 1

Para. 2

Para. 3

Para. 4

Para. 5

Para. 6

Para. 7

Para. 8

Para. 9

Unit 4　Manners

III. Judge, according to the text, whether the following statements are true or false. For false statements, write the facts in parentheses.

1. Parents strive to teach their children "good manners", only because they want their children to be polite.
   (　　　　　　　　　　　　　　　　　　　　　　　　　　　　　)
2. Parents are models for their children.
   (　　　　　　　　　　　　　　　　　　　　　　　　　　　　　)
3. Parents teach their children "good manners" mainly by telling them what to do or what to say.
   (　　　　　　　　　　　　　　　　　　　　　　　　　　　　　)
4. Different cultures have different social expectations towards people in that culture.
   (　　　　　　　　　　　　　　　　　　　　　　　　　　　　　)
5. An appropriate behavior in one culture is also acceptable in another culture since the world is evolving into a global community.
   (　　　　　　　　　　　　　　　　　　　　　　　　　　　　　)

IV. Paraphrase, use your own words to explain these sentences in the text with the help of the context.

1. (Para. 1) In a world full of obstacles, that is sometimes tumultuous, the concept of treating other human beings with kindness and of meeting social expectations is still among the basic skills parents are expected to teach their children.
   _____
   _____

2. (Para. 3) By setting a good example, parents are demonstrating to their children that if they say these phrases they will, more than likely, get what they want as a result of showing politeness.
   _____
   _____

3. (Para. 4) Since etiquette exists to satisfy and achieve social acceptance, a child lacking these skills will grow up to be socially clumsy and ostracised.
   _____
   _____

4. (Para. 5) Children pass through many stages from birth to adulthood, and

during these stages, parents are saddled with the enormous task of redirecting their children's selfish, self-gratifying actions into those of thoughtful, respectful little human beings.

_____
_____

5. (Para. 6) Only once children realize that others possess emotions and are able to foresee the consequence of their actions will an authentic attitude of respect develop.

_____
_____

6. (Para. 8) If children misbehave in public, whether accompanied by their parents or alone, it is a typical practice for an adult to correct them and even reprimand them on the spot in a way which would cause offence in America.

_____
_____

7. (Para. 9) It is far too common that the basic attitude of tolerance and respect is set aside or abandoned, and the result is chaos or even blood-shed.

_____
_____

Vocabulary Exercises

I. **Fill in each blank with one of the two words from each pair and note the difference of meaning between them. Change the form when necessary.**

1. APPROPRIATE   PROPER
   A. His formal style of speaking was _____ to the occasion.
   B. Her mother urged her to eat _____ meals instead of chips and biscuits.
2. GENUINE   REAL
   A. Our tour guide is a _____ Hawaiian.
   B. That kind of romance only happens in films, not in _____ life.
   C. He later told me the _____ reason for his absence.
   D. Is the painting a _____ Picasso?

3. PERCEPTIVE   PERSPECTIVE
   A. His mother's death gave him a new _____ on life.
   B. The most _____ of the three, she was the first to realize the potential danger of their situation.
   C. We need to view the problem in the proper _____.
   D. Just as a lamp can illuminate a dark room, a _____ comment can illuminate a knotty problem.
4. DISPLAY   DEMONSTRATE
   A. The children's work was _____ on the wall.
   B. The research findings clearly _____ the proposition.
   C. What are the workers _____ against outside of the governmental building?
   D. All the musicians _____ considerable skill as international masters.

II. **Choose a word or phrase that best completes each of the following sentences.**
   1. These enzymes _____ food in the stomach.
      A. break down   B. break in   C. break into   D. break through
   2. The company is being questioned _____ its employment policy.
      A. at   B. in   C. regarding   D. in term
   3. A huge amount of environmental damage has been _____ by the destruction of the rainforests.
      A. brought down   B. brought about   C. brought up   D. brought back
   4. Imports continue _____ a steady pace.
      A. in   B. on   C. through   D. at
   5. We should _____ some time each day for exercise.
      A. set about   B. set aside   C. set down   D. set back

III. **Fill in the blank in each sentence with a word or phrase taken from the box in its appropriate form.**

round the clock	result in	mimic	strive
consistently	owing to	perspective	

   1. The scientists _____ for a breakthrough in cancer research.
   2. The actor amused the audience by _____ some well-known people.
   3. The last five years has seen a _____ improvement in our country's economy.

4. Most literature on the subject of immigrants in France has been written from the _____ of the French themselves.

5. Acting before thinking always _____ failure.

6. Our trading connection has broken off _____ a disagreement over prices.

7. Surgeons are working _____ to save his life.

Translation Exercises

Translate each of the following sentences into English, using the word or phrase given in the brackets.

1. 每当老人忆起南京大屠杀的场景时,都难以平复内心的愤怒。(smooth)

2. 年轻人与老年人之间产生代沟的原因之一是因为他们认为年轻人的行为方式难以接受。(acceptable)

3. 为了使我们学起来更容易,在表演了整段舞蹈后,她把整个舞蹈分成了几个部分。(break into)

4. 虽然他们是孪生兄弟,但性格和爱好却有很大的差异。(differ in)

5. 找工作时,面试的第一印象很重要。因此,为了给未来的雇主留下好印象,面试时一定要注意举止和谈吐。(leave a(n) ... impression on)

6. 从长远来看,保护环境和减少温室气体排放量有助于中国经济的可持续发展。(in the long run)

7. 他的建议与公司的长期发展目标一致,受到了董事会的高度赞赏。(in harmony with)

8. 一旦飞机起飞,航空公司就要对乘客的安全负法律责任。(be responsible for)

Text II

My Chinese Canadian Family

> *Pre-reading Questions*
> 1. What does the phrase "Chinese-Canadian" mean?
> 2. If you go to a foreign country, what problems will you confront?

1 Chinese culture is very strong, rooted in thousands of years of history. It is no wonder that those of Chinese ethnicity born overseas are still considered Chinese no matter how localized they have become. When I visited China in 2004, I was warmly welcomed back to my ancestors' homeland with open arms, which brought significant closure to my life and identity. It is a long story that began before I was born.

2 The first wave of Chinese immigrants came to Canada as early as the 1860s for the gold rush and later to build Canada's cross-country railroad. These early immigrants experienced hardship in physical labour and racism in the form of prejudiced government policies and daily social interactions.

3 In 1967, immigration policies changed allowing another wave of Chinese to land in Canada. This group consisted mainly of educated professionals seeking a new life in Canada. Further changes to immigration policies in 1978 and 1985 saw an influx of wealthy Chinese from Hong Kong and Taiwan. The latest wave of immigration has seen more middle-class white collar workers immigrate to Canada, particularly from the Chinese mainland.

4 My parents came to Canada during the late 1960s as physicians. They were eager to leave bitter memories in Hong Kong for a new start to life in Canada. Both started life in Eastern Canada. My dad did his medical residency in Montreal while my mom finished her internship in Ottawa. They were married in 1969 and moved to Vancouver on Canada's

west coast one year later.

Then in 1973, I was born, a first-generation Chinese Canadian. Some call us "CBCs", short for Canadian-born Chinese. Others call us "bananas", those who have yellow skin on the outside, but are really more Western in upbringing and behaviour than Chinese. Of course, I had no idea about these terms when I was a little boy. I was just a kid growing up in the context I was born, unaware of the multitude of conflicts I would soon face growing up bicultural—Chinese and Canadian at the same time.

Until I was five years old, I spoke nothing but Cantonese, the language of our home. I played with other kids in pre-school without any problem. When I started kindergarten, I became aware that I could not communicate with my classmates. Somewhere along the way, I learned to speak English to the point I forgot my Cantonese. Every day in school, I would speak nothing but English, and then soon enough, I would also speak only English at home. My dad started to speak English with me, while my mother continued to use Cantonese, interspersed with English.

When I was in pre-school, I never saw any difference between my schoolmates and me. We were all just kids having fun. However when I was in grade school, I became painfully aware of my differences. Kids started to call me names like "chink" or "flat face". They occasionally beat me up, mockingly asking if I knew kung fu. (It's too bad I didn't know kung fu, so I could have defended myself!) It seemed that every difference in me was a target for bullying.

These differences were primarily born out of my upbringing as a Chinese born in Canada. The Chinese influence from my parents began to clash with the Canadian culture around me. Let me say, most importantly, that my parents were wonderful people with big hearts, somewhat bicultural themselves because of the British influence in Hong Kong. They never intended me any harm and raised me in the best way they knew. They could not fully understand my struggles at school because I would not have been able to explain what was happening, and they had their own problems to address.

As doctors, my parents had achieved what many Chinese parents wanted for their children. My parents had worked hard to become physicians and strived to succeed in their careers with the same determination. They desired excellence, bordering on perfection at times. Through their example, I learned to be hardworking, serious, quiet, and skillful at whatever I did. They rarely directly told me what they expected of me, but as the first-born son, I knew that I need to perform to their expectations, or risk disappointing them. They only wanted what was best for me. After all, their parents had done the same for them touting education as the key to success and security.

However at school, these values got me into trouble. My scholastic bent was not well received in a Canadian culture that valued athletic prowess. I was often labeled a "nerd" or a "geek" among other insults. I was mocked terribly after answering "I like classical music" when asked my musical tastes. My quiet nature, characteristic of many of the earlier Chinese immigrants, was interpreted as mentally slow, until they saw my exam scores. I wasn't very social and could not take jokes—all I saw was seriousness at home.

Why didn't I take a stand against any of this prejudice? I never understood it at the time, but now I can identify it as the typical Chinese non-confrontational approach, the desire to be humble, unassuming and harmony-seeking inherited from my parents.

Regardless of what happened at school, my parents were determined to make my younger brother and me successful. In return for high grades, we were given all the toys and material things we could want and were spoiled no end. My parents also did not want to repeat the harsh discipline they received as children, so we were never spanked and often got away with temper tantrums and complaining.

I was six years older than my brother. At times, I was his older brother watching out for him while at other times, I was his best friend having all sorts of fun. I tried to shield him from the racism and the conflicting cultural perspectives of my parents. With a much more relaxed personality than me, he turned out very balanced.

There were times in high school I wanted to be more independent, but my parents usually perceived this as interfering with my studies. One time, I looked for a job at a restaurant and became a dishwasher. After the second late night of work, my dad decided that I should not work and gave me more allowance money so I would stay home and study harder.

By the time I finished high school, I was like many CBC's in the same state—we were clueless about what we wanted to do in life, afraid to make choices, content just to stay at home where everything had been provided. My parents' desire to see me succeed as a doctor in their footsteps was thwarted as I barely

knew how to live as a young adult in society. I had been sheltered from many of the hardships my parents faced, but in doing this, I did not learn to develop the character needed to function more effectively in society.

16   The irony is that all the hardships my parents tried to shield me from, I have experienced through the "school of life" as an adult. At times it has been tough to learn basic life skills as an adult rather than as a youngster, but the journey has had its sweet moments as well. I've learned to appreciate the deep cultural heritage my parents gave me—the ability to understand the Chinese culture, enjoy Chinese food, approach life with Chinese work ethic, and many other things.

17   And it is with great thankfulness that I have been able to embrace the Chinese culture that was once the source of so much pain. Now I can see that one's cultural heritage does not determine one's worth, and I am free to explore the many facets of my ancestors' world as a part of my identity.

(1,398 words)

Reading Comprehension

I. **Answer the following questions with the information you got from the passage.**

1. What are the reasons for the Chinese immigration to Canada?
2. What was the first-generation Chinese Canadian called?
3. What cultural conflicts did the author encounter? And how did he solve the problems?
4. How did the way the father instructed the son influence the son's future life?

II. **Topics for discussion and reflection.**

1. How does culture shock influence immigrants' life?
2. How do people adapt to foreign culture? Is it easy to do? Why or why not?

Exercises for Integrated Skills

I. **Dictation**

   Listen to the following passage. Altogether the passage will be read to you four times. During the first reading, which will be read at normal speed, *listen and try to understand the meaning. For the second and third readings, the passage will be read sentence by sentence, or phrase by phrase, with intervals of 15 to 20 seconds. The last reading will be done at normal speed again and during this time you should check your work. You will then be given 2 minutes to check through your work once more.*

_____

_____

_____

_____

_____

II. Cloze

Fill in each blank in the passage below with a word or phrase taken from the box in its appropriate form.

> formal   housewarming   occasion   wear out   obligate
> beat   nicety   take   hospitable   token
> custom   compliment   snoop

An American friend has invited you to visit his family. You've never been to an American's home before, and you're not sure what to do. Should you __1__ a gift? How should you dress? What time should you arrive? What should you do when you get there? Glad you asked. When you're the guest, you should just make yourself at home. That's what __2__ is all about: making people feel at home when they're not.

The question of whether or not to bring a gift often makes guests squirm. Giving your host a gift is not just a social __3__ in some cultures—it's expected. But in American culture, a guest is not __4__ to bring a present. Of course, some people do bring a small __5__ of appreciation to their host. Appropriate gifts for general __6__ might be flowers, candy or—if the family has small children—toys. If you choose not to bring a gift, don't worry. No one will even notice.

American hospitality begins at home—especially when it involves food. Most Americans agree that good home cooking __7__ restaurant food any day.

When invited for a meal, you might ask, "Can I bring anything?" Unless it's a potluck, where everyone brings a dish, the host will probably respond, "No, just yourself." For most ___8___ dinners, you should wear comfortable, casual clothes. Plan to arrive on time, or else call to inform your hosts of the delay. During the dinner conversation, it's ___9___ to compliment the hostess on the wonderful meal. Of course, the biggest ___10___ is to eat lots of food!

When you've had plenty, you might offer to clear the table or wash the dishes. But since you're the guest, your hosts may not let you. Instead, they may invite everyone to move to the living room for dessert with tea or coffee. After an hour or so of general chit-chat, it's probably time to head for the door. You don't want to ___11___ your welcome. And above all, don't go ___12___ around the house. It's more polite to wait for the host to offer you a guided tour. But except for ___13___, guests often don't get past the living room.

Oral Activities

Activity One

Class Discussion: Do manners matter?

"Good manners will get you where you want to go faster than a speeding BMW," says an etiquette educator. According to some successful businessmen, "Good manners are good business." How far do you agree with these statements? Discuss whether manners can make a difference in your social life.

Activity Two

Class Discussion:

What are the differences between Western manners and Chinese manners?

Writing Practice

Note Writing: Introduction Note

You've just moved into a new house in the suburban district. You'd like to hold a party on the coming Saturday afternoon. Write a note to your friends and invite them to attend your party. You should write in about 60 words.

Unit 4 Manners

September ____

Dear all,

Angela and Jack

Passage Writing:

Good manners are helpful for you to succeed in business and social situations, but ways of expressing good manners are different from country to country. What are considered to be good manners in your country or hometown? Use one or two examples to illustrate your points. You should write about 80 words.

Unit 5 Leisure and Sports

Warm-up Activities

1. What do you do to pass time?
2. Suppose you are working in a hotel as a host or receptionist. Introduce the sports and leisure facilities (such as swimming pool, gymnasium, etc.) in your hotel to the guests.

Text I

Game

Pre-reading Questions

1. What are your favorite games? Do you think they are passive or active? Why?
2. What benefits can people gain from playing games?

1   Did you know that over 10 million people in the world regularly play chess? Millions more regularly play other games such as board games, card games, computer games, dice games, internet games, party games, video games, role-playing games, tile games, yard and deck games, fantasy games, trivia and word games, war games, and of course millions of people faithfully work crossword puzzles every day. Games are of great interest to people. Games are also of great interest to scientists. For example, mathematicians and computer programmers use games to help solve particular analyses. Psychologists and psychiatrists use games, such as psychodrama, as a therapeutic tool.

2   So what is the connection between games and the nature of leisure? One clue

Unit 5　Leisure and Sports

may be the origin of the word. The English word *game* is related to the old German word *gaman*, which means glee. Thus, the original meaning of the word game is not far from that of play—spontaneous, non-serious, and gleeful expression. Increasingly, however, social scientists have assigned  game a different meaning from play. Game today refers to a more structured, organized, and regulated form of activity.

3   A game is a contest. It may be a contest with yourself, such as the card game solitaire, or occur between two or more people or teams. Without the prospect of winning or losing, games lose some of their appeal. Even in tic-tac-toe, each participant wishes to win. Through cunning, manipulation, logic, luck, or even cooperation, the desired outcome is winning.

4   This means that a game must have rules. This is what distinguishes games as simple or complex; the more complex the rules, the more complex the game. In watching children play a game, you may notice how the rules are often casually developed (and changed) as the game goes along. Other games require not only a rulebook, but also a referee to interpret and apply the rules.

5   There are other characteristics of games. For example, games can be classified according to whether they require a particular place: a special table, field, room, or court. Other games are played anywhere the players meet (including over the Internet). Another characteristic of games is the use of particular equipment. While some games, such as tag, require no equipment, others require cards, dice, markers, a racquet, a board, a ball, or some other tools. Some professionalized games require a great deal of socialized equipment, as well as special rooms to store it.

6   A third characteristic of games is a specific time span. Time, in other words, often dictates who wins. Such games as charades or basketball are focused on beating the clock. Other games, such as Monopoly, are relatively indifferent to time, and can in fact, last for days.

7   Another, and perhaps the most important characteristic of games is that they are in some way artificial. They take place as a synthetic counterpart to real life. The contest of the chess match is the artificial enactment of a medieval war.

71

Monopoly is the counterfeit experience of capitalism.

8   The type of play required in a game, which is distinguished into agon, alea, mimicry, and ilinx, is the final characteristic. Agon, which means competitive, includes most sports and games, such as football and checkers. Alea games require luck, and wining is a matter of fate. Mimicry games involve role-playing, such as the game "sparks". Ilinx games involve vertigo and other sensory stimulation, such as hang gliding and drug use. When many people think of games, they usually think of only agon-type games.

9   Thanks to the categorization, we understand that games have a much wider range of meaning. The distinctions have also been useful in describing contemporary and sometimes harmful uses of games—drinking games, for example.

(611 words)

Words and Expressions

board game		桌面游戏，棋类游戏
dice game		a game that uses or incorporates a die as its sole or central component, usually as a random device 骰子游戏，投骰游戏
party game		a game which shares several features suitable to entertaining a social gathering of moderate size 派对游戏
video game		a game that involves interaction with a user interface to generate visual feedback on a video device 电子游戏
role-playing game		a type of game in which the participants (usually) assume the roles of characters acting in a fictional setting 角色扮演游戏
tile game		(麻将等)牌类游戏
deck	/dek/	n. a wooden floor built out from the back of a house, where you can sit and relax outdoors 露台
yard and deck game		庭院游戏
fantasy game		梦幻游戏
trivia	/ˈtrɪvjə/	n. detailed facts about history, sport, famous people, etc. 琐事
trivia game		难题问答游戏

Unit 5　Leisure and Sports

war game			a game that simulates or represents a military operation 模拟作战游戏
crossword puzzle			a word game in which you write the answers to questions in a pattern of numbered boxes 纵横字谜
mathematician	/ˌmæθɪməˈtɪʃən/	n.	a person skilled or learned in mathematics 数学家
programmer	/ˈprəʊɡræmə/	n.	someone whose job is to write computer programs 程序设计员
psychologist	/saɪˈkɒlədʒɪst/	n.	someone who is trained in psychology 心理学家
psychiatrist	/saɪˈkaɪətrɪst/	n.	a doctor trained in the treatment of mental illness 精神病医生
psychodrama	/ˈsaɪkəʊˌdrɑːmə/	n.	a way of treating mental illness in which people are asked to act in a situation together to help them understand their emotions 心理表演治疗法
therapeutic	/ˌθerəˈpjuːtɪk/	adj.	relating to the treatment or cure of an illness 治疗的
clue	/kluː/	n.	something that serves to guide or direct in the solution of a problem or mystery 线索
glee	/gliː/	n.	a feeling of satisfaction and excitement 欣喜，高兴 **gleeful** adj. 欣喜的
spontaneous	/spɒnˈteɪmjəs/	adj.	(of something) happening by itself, not planned or organized 自然的，自发的
structured	/ˈstrʌktʃəd/	adj.	carefully organized, planned, or arranged 精心安排的
regulated	/ˈreɡjʊleɪtɪd/	adj.	controlled by rules 有管理规则的
contest	/ˈkɒntest/	n.	a competition 竞赛
solitaire	/ˌsɒlɪˈteə/	n.	a game played by one person with small wooden or plastic pieces on a board 单人纸牌戏
tic-tac-toe	/ˈtɪk-tæk-ˌtəʊ/	n.	a children's game in which two players draw X's or O's in a pattern of nine squares, trying to get three in a row "连城"游戏
cunning	/ˈkʌnɪŋ/	adj.	clever but often dishonest 狡猾的，巧妙的
manipulation	/məˌnɪpjʊˈleɪʃən/	n.	working skilfully with information, systems, etc. to achieve the result that you want 操纵
interpret	/ɪnˈtɜːprɪt/	vt.	to explain the meaning of something 解释
tag	/tæɡ/	n.	a children's game in which one player chases and tries to touch the others 捉人游戏
racquet	/ˈrækɪt/	n.	a specially shaped piece of wood or metal that has a circle filled with tight strings at one end, used for

			hitting the ball in games such as tennis 球拍
professionalize	/prəˈfeʃənəlaɪz/	vt.	to make professional 使专业化 **professionalized** adj. 专业化的
span	/spæn/	n.	a period of time between two dates or events 间隔, 期间
dictate	/dɪkˈteɪt/	vt.	to control or influence something 决定, 支配, 影响
charade	/ʃəˈrɑːd/	n.	a game in which one person uses actions and no words to show the meaning of a word or phrase, and other people have to guess what it is 看表演猜字谜游戏
Monopoly	/məˈnɒpəlɪ/	n.	a very popular type of board game that has been sold since the 1930s. Players use toy money to buy property and buildings on squares on the board, and then make other players pay rent if they move onto those squares. 大富翁游戏, 地产大亨游戏
synthetic	/sɪnˈθetɪk/	adj.	not natural or genuine; artificial or contrived 人造的
counterpart	/ˈkaʊntəpɑːt/	n.	someone or something that has a similar position or function to another in a different place 职能（或地位）相当的人, 对应的事物
enact	/ɪˈnækt/	vt.	to act in a play, story, etc. 扮演, 演出 **enactment** n. 演出
medieval	/ˌmedɪˈiːvəl/	adj.	connected with the Middle Ages 中世纪的
counterfeit	/ˈkaʊntəfɪt/	adj.	to made to look exactly like something else, in order to deceive people 伪造的, 假冒的
agon	/ˈægəʊn/	n.	a conflict 冲突
alea	/ˈeɪlɪə/	n.	the chance of gain or loss resulted from uncertainty 偶然性
mimicry	/ˈmɪmɪkrɪ/	n.	the action of mimicking someone or something 模仿
ilinx	/ɪˈlɪŋks/	n.	a kind of play which creates a temporary disruption of perception 发眩游戏
vertigo	/ˈvɜːtɪɡəʊ/	n.	a feeling of sickness and dizziness caused by looking down from a high place 眩晕的感觉
sensory	/ˈsensərɪ/	adj.	relating to or using your physical senses 感官的
stimulate	/ˈstɪmjʊleɪt/	vt.	to make active or more active 刺激, 使兴奋 **stimulation** n. 刺激; 激励

Unit 5 Leisure and Sports

hang gliding		n.	the sport of flying using a hang-glider (a large frame covered with cloth, which is used to fly from a high place without an engine, with the pilot hanging underneath) 悬挂式滑翔
categorize	/ˈkætɪɡəraɪz/	vt.	to put people or things into groups according to the type of person or thing they are 分类 **categorization** n. 分类

Reading Comprehension

I. Write down the main idea(s) for each part.

Part I   (Para(s).   ) _____.
Part II   (Para(s).   ) _____.
Part III   (Para(s).   ) _____.
   1. _____.
   2. _____.
   3. _____.
   4. _____.
   5. _____.
Part IV   (Para(s).   ) _____.

II. Answer the following questions.

1. What are the functions of games? Explain by providing examples.
2. What are the similarities and differences between the meaning of "glee" and "game"?
3. Why must a game have rules?
4. How would you define the word "artificial" in games?
5. According to the categorization in paragraph 8, what are the four types of play in games? Explain with examples.

III. **Judge, according to the text, whether the following statements are true or false. For false statements, write the facts in parentheses.**

1. There are more people playing crossword puzzles than those playing chess.
   ( )
2. Games without possibilities of winning or losing have little attractiveness.
   ( )
3. The complexity of a game is determined by its corresponding rules.
   ( )
4. Time often determines the winners of games such as charades, basketball, or Monopoly.
   ( )
5. When people think of games, they usually only think of competitive ones.
   ( )

IV. **Paraphrase, use your own words to explain the sentences in the text with the help of the context.**

1. (Para. 2) Thus, the original meaning of the word game is not far from that of play—spontaneous, non-serious, and gleeful expression.

2. (Para. 6) Such games as charades or basketball are focused on beating the clock.

3. (Para. 7) They take place as a synthetic counterpart to real life.

4. (Para. 8) Ilinx games involve vertigo and other sensory stimulation, such as hang gliding and drug use.

5. (Para. 9) Thanks to the categorization, we understand that games have a much wider range of meaning.

Unit 5　Leisure and Sports

Vocabulary Exercises

I. Choose a word or phrase that best completes each of the following sentences.

1. Whoever formulated the theory of the origin of the universe, it is just _____ and needs proving.
   A. spontaneous　　B. hypothetical　　C. intuitive　　D. empirical
2. The problem is that most local authorities lack the _____ to deal sensibly in this market.
   A. anticipation　　B. perception　　C. prospect　　D. expertise
3. He made another wonderful discovery, _____ of great importance to science.
   A. which I think is　　　　　　B. which I think it is
   C. which I think it　　　　　　D. I think which is
4. There have been _____ few plane crashes this year.
   A. relative　　B. related　　C. relate　　D. relatively
5. Acupuncture is the _____ of thin metallic needles inserted into anatomically defined locations on the body to affect bodily function.
   A. supervision　　B. manipulation　　C. regulation　　D. coordination
6. The early pioneers had to _____ many hardships to settle on the new land.
   A. go along　　B. go back on　　C. go through　　D. go into
7. The game will be played _____ rules laid down for the 1992 Cup.
   A. according to　　B. according　　C. according as　　D. depending on
8. _____ the generosity of the public, we've reached our goal of $50,000.
   A. Thanks to　　B. Owing to　　C. Due to　　D. Because of
9. Nathaniel Hawthorne was one of those who were _____ to transcendentalism.
   A. optimistic　　B. indifferent　　C. pessimistic　　D. enthusiastic

II. Fill in the blank in each sentence with a word taken from the box in its appropriate form.

| therapeutic | enactment | regulate | counterfeit | interpret |
| synthetic | glee | stimulation | contemporary | sensory |

1. This _____ dress material does not crush.
2. Some people claim that herbs have _____ value for treating pain.
3. To make easy money, a number of stores knowingly sell _____ items.
4. Your _____ and motor nerve cells can sometimes work together without involving your brain.
5. All company staff must comply with the _____.
6. She danced with _____ when she saw the new toys, which her father bought for her birthday.
7. This book is about the life of a _____ Chinese writer.
8. Her refusal to work late was _____ as a lack of commitment to the company.
9. The activities are designed to _____ classroom discussions.
10. Congress barred the door to any attempt to _____ a new tax law.

Translation Exercises

Translate each of the following sentences into English, using the word or phrase given in the brackets.

1. 在打捞失事轮船的过程中,我们没发现什么值钱的东西,不过打捞出来的众多物品还是引起了我们极大的兴趣。(of great interest)

2. 求职屡次受挫后,他越来越频繁地用消极的方式谈论工作。(increasingly)

3. 雾太浓的时候,即便你用望远镜也不能把100米以内的村庄和森林区分开来。(distinguish)

4. 运动员一出现在跑道上,观众就自发地热烈欢呼。(spontaneous)

5. 图书管理员把收藏的书刊分类编成目录后,就可以在图书馆的电脑上迅速查找到我们需要的书籍。(classify)

6. 学习一门新技术时,最初你或许会遇到一些困难,但坚持下去就会觉得越来越容易。(go along)

___

7. 他虽在闹市区上班,但工作时总能思想高度集中,从不在意外面的喧嚣。(indifferent to)

___

8. 本次奥运会上,中国女排需要打败数个强劲对手,才能赢得冠军。(counterpart)

___

Text II
Leisure-time Activities—Picture and Sound

Pre-reading Questions
1. What are some leisure-time activities Americans have?
2. What are the pros and cons of TV?

1   At one time, leisure meant resting, relaxing, doing nothing, sitting on the front porch swing and watching the world go by. Today, however, most Americans cram a lot of activities into their so-called leisure time. They may perform these activities to become physically fit, learn something new, do something creative, bring the family closer together, or have a great adventure. Having fun, of course, is another goal. But many Americans take their leisure pursuits quite seriously; they hope these activities will enrich their lives in some way.

2   By far, the most popular leisure-time activity is watching television. There is at least one TV set in 98% of American households, and many have two or three. About 82% of American homes have a videocassette recorder (VCR), which is capable of recording and playing back TV shows or movies.

3   What's on TV? Afternoon programming consists mostly of game shows, talk shows, and never-ending dramas commonly called *soap operas*. For children,

daytime TV offers clever programs that educate while entertaining. There are also a lot of cartoons. At dinner time, news is broadcast. Evening entertainment consists mostly of situation comedies (sitcoms), which portray some aspects of life (families, singles, seniors, and so on) in a humorous way. There are also movies, adventure shows, dramas, and various weekly shows  with the same cast of characters and general theme but a different story each week.

4   For those who want more TV than the free stations provide, cable TV is available in most parts of the country. To receive cable TV, one must pay a monthly subscription fee. Wires are attached to the TV set to enable the subscriber to receive the cable broadcasts. Cable channels tend to specialize in one type of program. There are stations for news, sports, movies, music videos, business, health, history, and the arts.

5   TV, at its best, is entertaining and educational. However, there are two problems: Most viewers watch too much, and the quality (especially on the free stations) is often poor. How much is too much? Studies indicate that the average American watches TV about 28 hours a week. (Children watch about 20 hours; older women are up to 42 hours.) According to one study in 1950, American 14-year-olds had a vocabulary of 25,000 words, but today's children the same age know only 10,000 words. The reason for the decrease may be that TV takes up a lot of leisure time kids once spent reading. Technology will continue to offer consumers bigger TV screens and clearer pictures at affordable prices. Moreover, TV of the future will be more interactive. (Viewers will have more control over the action.) Better technical quality may encourage viewers to watch even more—and, some say, become even less physically fit and more overweight.

6   And what about quality? On the commercial networks especially, many shows are silly, trite, in poor taste, or extremely violent. By the age of 18, the typical American has seen 40,000 killings on TV and in movies combined. Does all this fake bloodshed cause some teens to commit real violent crimes? Some

people think there's a connection. American TV has earned the insulting nicknames "boob tube" and "idiot box". But for those who want to avoid either too much TV or bad TV, the solution is simple: click the "off" button.

7   Movies are another common source of entertainment, viewed in theaters or at home. TV stations show movies, and there is a store that rents videotapes or DVDs in just about every neighborhood. Americans consume movies in great quantities, and movie stars become public idols. Once a year, the movie industry gives out a whole series of honors to movie-makers. Nearly a billion people worldwide watch this televised awards presentation—the Academy Awards.

8   Other popular sources of entertainment are recordings and radio. Sales of recordings in all forms (compact discs and audiocassettes) exceed $ 12 billion annually, with compact discs by far the most popular medium. Radio, too, has its place in the American entertainment scene. It's a great companion in the car, on the treadmill, or on the jogging trail.

(676 words)

Reading Comprehension

I. **Answer the following questions with the information taken from the passage.**
   1. What benefits can Americans gain from leisure activities?
   2. Based on the article, what are the categories for different TV programs?
   3. What are some problems with American TV?
   4. Make a list of sources of entertainment mentioned in the article.

II. **Topics for discussion and reflection.**
   1. How does an individual's level of education influence their choice of leisure activities?
   2. Do you prefer to spend your free time outdoors or indoors, why?

Exercises for Integrated Skills

I. **Dictation**

   Listen to the following passage. Altogether the passage will be read to you four times. During the first reading, which will be read at normal speed, listen and try to understand the meaning. For the second and third readings, the passage will be read sentence by sentence, or phrase by phrase, with intervals of 15 to 20 seconds. The last reading will be done at normal speed again and during this time you should check your work. You will then be given 2 minutes to check through your work once more.

_____
_____
_____
_____

II. **Cloze**

Fill in each blank in the passage below with a word taken from the box in its appropriate form.

promote	prevent	score	myth	batter
profession	leisure	alternate	inning	metaphor
establish	govern	trace	pitch	ancestor

Baseball

Various bat-and-ball games have been played in many parts of the world for ages, but it is difficult to ___1___ the origins of modern-day baseball. Some point to the Irish game of "rounders" as the possible ___2___, but there are other candidates as well. Baseball as we know it today developed in mid-19th-century America. By 1869, the first ___3___ baseball club was formed. In the late 19th century and early 20th century, two American leagues—the National League and the American League—were formed. In 1903, the World Series was ___4___ as a competition between the champions of the two leagues. Thus, Major League Baseball was formed.

Baseball is played by two teams of nine players. The teams ___5___, with a member of one of the teams hitting the ball with a bat and the other team catching and ___6___ the ball. The hitting team ___7___ by having a player run across the four "bases" on the baseball field that form what is called a "diamond." The player is able to run when the ___8___ hits the ball. The pitching team uses various tactics (striking out, forcing out, tagging, or catching the ball in the air) to   9   the batting team from scoring a run. A professional or college baseball game lasts for nine "   10   ." In each inning each team member has one turn to bat and to score "runs" before it makes three "outs." Baseball is one of the few sports not   11   by a clock.

Baseball is popular throughout North America, Central America, the Caribbean and some parts of East Asia. American Major League Baseball has numerous players from Latin America and some from East Asia, especially Japan. Known for its   12   pace, punctuated by dramatic climaxes, it has an almost   13   place in popular American culture. Considered a quintessential American game, it has been depicted in numerous works of literature and film as a   14   for life's dreams and sudden turns of fortune. Baseball also has been used to   15   civil rights, for example by Jackie Robinson, who in 1947 integrated baseball by becoming the first African-American to play in the major leagues.

Oral Activities

1. Top five most popular games

Work in groups of 4–5 to make a list of games you play for fun during your leisure time. Be sure to include the rules as well. Share your collections with other groups and then vote for the top five most popular games in the class.

2. The best childhood leisure activities

Many adults have forgotten that the best way to relax is to play like kids. Recall your childhood games and share your fondest activities with your classmates.

3. Free leisure activities

Many people equate leisure activities with money. Movies, concerts, and shows are exciting and enjoyable but may cost a lot. With imagination and a spirit of adventure you can find good leisure activities at no cost at all. In groups, discuss and list various forms of free leisure activities.

Writing Practice

Note Writing:

Your birthday is coming, so you would like to have a picnic with your best friends in the park this Sunday. Write a note to your roommate, Lily, and ask her to join your picnic. Your note should have the following parts:

1) Date
2) Salutation
3) Body
4) Signature.

Write no more than 60 words.

Sept. _____

Dear Lily,

Yours always,
Jenny

Paragraph Writing:

Write a paragraph on either of the following two topics. In your paragraph use at least 6 words or phrases from the list below. Write at least 150 words.

1) My Favorite Pastime
2) How People Spend Their Leisure Time

relaxation	laughter	fashion	universal	entertainment
appeal to	enjoyment	recreation	talk-show	movie
make fun of	chess	drama	age group	healthy
rewarding	thrill	sports	outdoor activities	
cross-talk (comic dialogue)				

Unit 6 Happiness

Warm-up Activities

1. Do you believe a happiness pill will fill you with energy and joy for life?
2. Interviews: Below is a question and several unfinished statements about personal happiness. Take turns asking your partner and write down the answers with key words only.

Question and statements	Your partner's answers
What/Who is responsible for your happiness?	
If you had more _____ you could be happier.	
You will be happy when _____.	
People who are happy smile a lot. True/False.	
Happiness is easy to achieve. True/False.	
One of the most important things to do to find lasting happiness is _____.	
Happy people have as many problems as unhappy people. True/False.	
Happy people live for _____. Unhappy people live for _____.	

Now report your partner's answers to the class.

Text I

The Science of Happiness

> **Pre-reading Questions**
>
> 1. Do you think you are a happy person? What are some ways to make a person happy and positive in life?
> 2. Do you agree that happiness is mostly genetic? Why or why not?

1   Are you living a productive and meaningful life? Do you work on a cause that is important to you? Are you really passionate about something and are you bringing your personal strengths to bear on it? Do you know why you are here? Do you feel you are going somewhere wholeheartedly?

2   According to the psychologist Martin Seligman, author of *Authentic Happiness*, if you answer these questions in the affirmative, chances are that you are already a happy person.

3   Recent studies have shown that subjective well-being depends little on such "good things" of life as health, wealth, good looks or social status. Happiness seems to relate more directly to how you live your life with what you have.

4   Remember the "set point" theory about personal weight? The theory claimed that loss of weight is a temporary phenomenon. For example, people diet and lose weight for a while but in a given time, they tend to come back to their usual weight.

5   The set-point theory seems to apply to happiness as well. We tend to gravitate around our usual level of happiness. So there you are. You already knew you had a thermostat in your car and your house and now you know you have a "happiness thermostat" in your mind to adjust the "ups and downs" caused by life events.

6   Let me give two examples to illustrate this point: 1) Able-bodied people who suddenly become paraplegic; 2) Lottery winners who become wealthy overnight. People, in both examples, in spite of their changed circumstances, one in a wheel chair and the other with millions in the bank, return to their previous level of happiness (or unhappiness) within a year. Isn't that fascinating? Human be-

ings are not slaves to their circumstances, after all!

7   However, current research also shows that mood and temperament are partially determined by genetics. From this we can conclude that genes have a hand in determining the level of our happiness, but circumstances don't, barring a few exceptions, of course. For example, extreme poverty for an indefinitely long period can affect the level of happiness.

8   If you feel discouraged because you were not born with an abundance of happy genes, take heart. Remember, genes play a partial role in the degree of happiness you are capable of experiencing, but genes don't determine all of it. Genes simply offer you a range to work with. It's up to you whether you operate at the top end or the bottom end of the range of your happiness.

9   To use another analogy, say you live in a house you inherit from your parents. It's up to you which part of the house you live in. You may live in the basement where it's dark and dingy or, the top floor of the house, which is light and bright and has a great view of the ocean.

10   Desire can help us or hurt us. It is helpful when desire moves us to achieve positive and worthy goals. But, desire can become infinite and unappeasable. Unrestrained desire can become a constant source of unhappiness. Therefore, at some point of materialistic gains and self-fulfillment, contentment and gratification are necessary to maintain a level of happiness.

11   Gratification is derived from rising to the challenges posed by your family, work and other responsibilities or duties. But, in order to be gratified, you have to be in a receptive mental mode.

12   Likewise, contentment does not result from a perfect job, perfect family or a perfect society. But, contentment is a result of your feeling that you are trying your best to make something perfect; when you feel that you are living a productive life.

13   What does it mean to live a productive life? When you know what your strengths are and you are putting them to good use.

14　　Make your job as your "calling" and your family as your "mission." Regard service to others as part of your self-fulfillment. Engage in the tasks that are consistent with your values and help you to take your skills and abilities to the next higher level.

15　　The more challenges you master and the more you utilize your personal strengths, the more the good feelings will permeate your life.

16　　The happiest people in the world are not those who have perfect lives, but the people who have learned to enjoy things that are less than perfect.

(719 words)

Words and Expressions

productive	/prəˈdʌktɪv/	*adj.*	having a good or useful result 富有成效的
passionate	/ˈpæʃənɪt/	*adj.*	having or expressing strong emotions 充满热情的
authentic	/ɔːˈθentɪk/	*adj.*	reliable and accurate 可靠的，准确的
affirmative	/əˈfɜːmətɪv/	*adj.*	indicating that you agree with what someone has said or that the answer to a question is 'yes' 肯定的
subjective	/səbˈdʒektɪv/	*adj.*	influenced by or based on personal beliefs or feelings, rather than based on facts 主观的
temporary	/ˈtempərəri/	*adj.*	lasting for only a limited period of time 暂时的
diet	/ˈdaɪət/	*vi.*	to limit the amount and type of food that you eat, in order to become thin 节食
apply	/əˈplaɪ/	*vi.*	to have an effect on or to concern a particular person, group, or situation **apply to** 适用
gravitate	/ˈɡrævɪteɪt/	*vi.*	to be attracted by or to move in the direction of something or someone (受)吸引
thermostat	/ˈθɜːməstæt/	*n.*	an instrument used for keeping a room or a machine at a particular temperature 温度调节装置
paraplegic	/ˌpærəˈpliːdʒɪk/	*adj.*	suffering complete paralysis of the lower half of the body usually resulting from damage to the spinal cord (患)截瘫的
lottery	/ˈlɒtəri/	*n.*	a game, often organized by the state or a charity in order to make money, in which numbered tickets are sold to people who then have a chance of winning a prize if their number is chosen 彩票
temperament	/ˈtempərəmənt/	*n.*	the emotional part of someone's character, espe-

			cially how likely they are to be happy, angry, etc. 性情
gene	/dʒiːn/	n.	a part of the DNA in a cell which contains information in a special pattern received by each animal or plant from its parents, and which controls its physical development, behaviour, etc. 基因
barring	/'bɑːrɪŋ/	prep.	unless something happens 除非
abundance	/ə'bʌndəns/	n.	a large quantity of something 丰富，充裕
analogy	/ə'nælədʒɪ/	n.	a comparison between things which have similar features, often used to help explain a principle or idea 类比
inherit	/ɪn'herɪt/	vt.	to have the same character or appearance as your parents 遗传而得
dingy	/'dɪndʒɪ/	adj.	dark, dirty, and in bad condition 暗黑的，邋遢的
infinite	/'ɪnfɪnɪt/	adj.	without limits; extremely large or great 无限的
unrestrained	/'ʌnrɪs'treɪnd/	adj.	not controlled or limited 无限制的
materialistic	/mə,tɪərɪə'lɪstɪk/	adj.	concerned only with money and possessions rather than things of the mind such as art, religion, or moral beliefs 唯物主义的，实利主义的
gratification	/,grætɪfɪ'keɪʃən/	n.	great satisfaction 满意
pose	/pəʊz/	vt.	to cause something, especially a problem or difficulty 引起，造成
receptive	/rɪ'septɪv/	adj.	willing to consider new ideas or listen to someone else's opinions 善于接受的，能接纳的
likewise	/'laɪk-waɪz/	adv.	in the same way 同样地
consistent	/kən'sɪstənt/	adj.	without contradiction 一致的
utilize	/'juːtɪlaɪz/	vt.	to use something for a particular purpose 利用
permeate	/'pɜːmɪeɪt/	vt.	to spread through and be present in every part of something 渗透

Reading Comprehension

I. Decide which of the following best states the author's writing purpose.

A. To stress the importance of happiness.

B. To inform the reader how to be happy.

C. To tell where happiness lies.

D. To introduce current research on the science of happiness.

II. Answer the following questions.

1. How can the set-point theory apply to happiness? Explain by providing examples.
2. What factors determine the level of happiness?
3. Why does the author say desire can help us and hurt us as well?
4. When do people feel they are living productive lives?
5. What does the author mean by saying, "The happiest people in the world are not those who have perfect lives, but the people who have learned to enjoy things that are less than perfect"?

III. Judge, according to the text, whether the following statements are true or false. For false statements, write the facts in parentheses.

1. Human well-being depends on health, wealth, good looks and social status.
   (   )
2. According to the set-point theory, people in the long run cannot lose weight.
   (   )
3. It is impossible for a person who loses a leg in an accident to return to his/her usual level of happiness.
   (   )
4. Gratification results from a perfect job, a perfect family and a perfect society.
   (   )
5. People can achieve self-fulfillment when they help others who are in trouble.
   (   )

IV. Paraphrase, use your own words to explain the sentences in the text with the help of the context.

1. (Para. 2) According to the psychologist Martin Seligman, author of *Authentic Happiness,* if you answer these questions in the affirmative, chances are that you are already a happy person.

2. (Para. 5) You already knew you had a thermostat in your car and your house and now you know you have a "happiness thermostat" in your mind to adjust the "ups and downs" caused by life events.

3. (Para. 7) From this we can conclude that genes have a hand in determining the level of our happiness, but circumstances don't, barring a few exceptions, of course.

4. (Para. 8) It's up to you whether you operate at the top end or the bottom end of the range of your happiness.

5. (Para. 10) Therefore, at some point of materialistic gains and self-fulfillment, contentment and gratification are necessary to maintain a level of happiness.

6. (Para. 14) Engage in the tasks that are consistent with your values and help you to take your skills and abilities to the next higher level.

7. (Para. 15) The more challenges you master and utilize your personal strengths, the more the good feelings will permeate your life.

Vocabulary Exercises

I. **Fill in each blank with one of the given words and note the difference of meaning between them. Change the form when necessary.**
   1. PREVIOUS   FORMER
      A. Putin stressed that the _____ Soviet Union was the first to establish

diplomatic relations with new China upon its founding.

B. There were almost no women MPs _____ to 1945. (MP: Member of Parliament)

C. The patient has no _____ history of attempted suicides.

2. CIRCUMSTANCE   SITUATION   STATE

A. With food supplies running out, the _____ in the flood-stricken area is getting desperate.

B. Under these _____ we have to admit that this is the best result that could be expected.

C. His girlfriend's death left him in a distressed _____ of mind.

D. In no _____ are you to leave the house after 12 o'clock for safety reasons.

3. ILLUSTRATE   EXPLAIN   CLARIFY

A. President Nixon's miserable downfall _____ the immense power of the media.

B. The general manager has _____ his position on equal pay for women staff in the latest conference.

C. The librarian will _____ how to use the catalogue system to the freshmen.

D. His story clearly _____ his generosity to the needy people.

4. WORTHY   WORTH   WORTHWHILE

A. It's _____ all the time and energy you have put in when you see from the top of the mountain.

B. I would rather my energy went to a _____ job.

C. *The Sound of Music* is really a film _____ seeing.

II. Choose a word or phrase that best completes each of the following sentences.

1. _____ the threat of war, he says he remains confident that peace is possible.
   A. In spite of   B. Out spite of   C. Inspite   D. Outspite

2. She was uncertain _____ to stay or leave.
   A. if   B. whether   C. /   D. that

3. The fish was delicious. _____, the eggplant was excellent.
   A. Wisely   B. Similar   C. Likewise   D. Likewisely

4. We are still dealing with problems _____ errors made in the past.
   A. resulting from   B. resulting in   C. result from   D. result in
5. The more I thought about it, _____ confused I became.
   A. more   B. less   C. most   D. the more

III. Fill in the blank in each sentence with a word or phrase taken from the box in its appropriate form.

> productive   illustrate   unappeasable   work on
> passionate   affirmative   apply   determine
> inherit   unrestrained   consistent

1. That outburst was _____ of her bad temper.
2. You may have a _____ for her, but it isn't love.
3. I want to find a job in which I can _____ my major.
4. He was furious, but his manner was very _____.
5. It was a blunder for them to try to _____ the aggressor.
6. In order to turn the deserts into fertile and _____ land, engineers built an 800-mile canal.
7. I appreciated the debaters on the _____ side in the debate.
8. The _____ of the regulation is not your business—your job is to follow it.
9. The large _____ from her uncle meant that she could buy her own boat.
10. The last five years have seen a(n) _____ improvement in the country's economy
11. In the next several years there can be ten different research groups _____ the project.

Translation Exercises

Translate each of the following sentences into English, using the word or phrase given in the brackets.

1. 虽然她在生活中遭受了一连串挫折,但仍对工作充满激情。(passionate about)

2. 作为校足球队里唯一的守门员,他必须全心全意地投入到这场比赛中去。(wholeheartedly)

3. 她的讲话与正在讨论的主题无关。(relate to)

4. 这个规则并不适用于所有的篮球比赛。(apply to)

5. 气馁的时候听听莫扎特的音乐,你会感到振奋。(discouraged)

6. 这个项目的成败取决于你们,所以你们一定要全力以赴。(up to)

7. 李明尽力说服妻子和他一起出国读书,但是他的努力终成泡影。(result from)

8. 他的言行不一致,很显然他在欺骗我们。(consistent with)

Text II

Ten Keys to Happiness

> **Pre-reading Questions**
>
> 1. Do do you think happiness is the most important thing in your life? Why or why not?
> 2. How do you define "happiness"? Why?

1   Physical wellbeing is inseparable from emotional wellbeing. Happy people are healthy people. The wisdom traditions of the world tell us that happiness does not depend on what you have, but on who you are. As we begin the new year, it may be worthwhile to reflect on what really creates happiness in us. The following ten keys, gleaned from the wisdom traditions, may give us some insights.

2   Listen to your body's wisdom, which expresses itself through signals of comfort and discomfort. When choosing a certain behavior, ask your body, "How

Unit 6 Happiness

do you feel about this?" If your body sends a signal of physical or emotional distress, watch out. If your body sends a signal of comfort and eagerness, proceed.

3 Live in the present, for it is the only moment you have. Keep your attention on what is here and now; look for the fullness in every moment. Accept what comes to you totally and completely so that you can appreciate it, learn from it, and then let it go. The present is as it should be. It reflects infinite laws of Nature that have brought you this exact thought, this exact physical response. This moment is as it is because the universe is as it is. Don't struggle against the infinite scheme of things; instead, be at one with it.

4 Take time to be silent, to meditate, to quiet the internal dialogue. In moments of silence, realize that you are re-contacting your source of pure awareness. Pay attention to your inner life so that you can be guided by intuition rather than externally imposed interpretations of what is or isn't good for you.

5 Relinquish your need for external approval. You alone are the judge of your worth, and your goal is to discover infinite worth in yourself, no matter what anyone else thinks. There is great freedom in this realization.

6 When you find yourself reacting with anger or opposition to any person or circumstance, realize that you are only struggling with yourself. Putting up resistance is the response of defenses created by old hurts. When you relinquish this anger, you will be healing yourself and cooperating with the flow of the universe.

7 Know that the world "out there" reflects your reality "in here." The people you react to most strongly, whether with love or hate, are projections of your inner world. What you most hate is what you most deny in yourself. What you most love is what you most wish for in yourself. Use the mirror of relationships to guide your evolution. The goal is total self-knowledge. When you achieve that, what you most want will automatically be there, and what you most dislike will disappear.

8 Shed the burden of judgment—you will feel much lighter. Judgment imposes right and wrong on situations that just are. Everything can be understood and forgiven, but when you judge, you cut off understanding and shut down the

process of learning to love. In judging others, you reflect your lack of self-acceptance. Remember that every person you forgive adds to your self-love.

9   Don't contaminate your body with toxins, either through food, drink, or toxic emotions. Your body is more than a life-support system. It is the vehicle that will carry you on the journey of your evolution. The health of every cell directly contributes to your state of wellbeing, because every cell is a point of awareness within the field of awareness that is you.

10   Replace fear-motivated behavior with love-motivated behavior. Fear is the product of memory, which dwells in the past. Remembering what hurt us before, we direct our energies toward making certain that an old hurt will not repeat itself. But trying to impose the past on the present will never wipe out the threat of being hurt. That happens only when you find the security of your own being, which is love. Motivated by the truth inside you, you can face any threat because your inner strength is invulnerable to fear.

11   Understand that the physical world is just a mirror of a deeper intelligence. Intelligence is the invisible organizer of all matter and energy, and since a portion of this intelligence resides in you, you share in the organizing power of the cosmos. Because you are inseparably linked to everything, you cannot afford to foul the planet's air and water. But at a deeper level, you cannot afford to live with a toxic mind, because every thought makes an impression on the whole field of intelligence. Living in balance and purity is the highest good for you and the Earth.

(773 words)

Reading Comprehension

I. Answer the following questions with the information you got from the passage.
   1. What is the relationship between happiness and health?
   2. How could a person listen to the body's wisdom?
   3. Do you think the tips that the author offers are practical or not? Why?
   4. Could you give us more tips on how to be a happy person?

II. Topics for discussion and reflection.
   1. Please discuss with your partners whether sports can build character or not.

2. What kind of life do you think is the happiest life? Why? Are you happy every day? Why or why not?

Exercises for Integrated Skills

I. Dictation

Listen to the following passage. Altogether the passage will be read to you four times. During the first reading, which will be read at normal speed, listen and try to understand the meaning. For the second and third readings, the passage will be read sentence by sentence, or phrase by phrase, with intervals of 15 to 20 seconds. The last reading will be done at normal speed again and during this time you should check your work. You will then be given 2 minutes to check through your work once more.

_____
_____
_____
_____
_____

II. Cloze

Fill in each blank in the passage below with a word taken from the box in its appropriate form.

achieve	produce	outward	advantage	answer
natural	misery	expose	capable	government
commit	worth	secrete	highly-paid	self-esteem

Many people think that when they become rich and successful, happiness will ___1___ follow. Let me tell you that certainly nothing is further from the truth. The world is full of very rich people who are as ___2___ as hell. We have all read stories about movie stars ___3___ suicide or dying from drugs. Quite clearly, money is not the ___4___ to all problems.

Wealth ___5___ through dishonest means does not bring happiness. Lottery winnings do not bring happiness. Wealth left by parents does not bring happiness. In fact, money alone is almost ___6___. If you have both ___7___ and money, however, you are well on the way to happiness. What is missing in both self-esteem and money is ___8___ work and a real contribution towards the happiness of others. The ___9___ to happiness lies in the contribution towards the happiness of others. You can fool others but you can never fool yourself. If you obtain wealth through luck or dishonest means, you will know you did not earn it. If you have taken ___10___ of or hurt others to earn your wealth, you will not be happy. You will not like yourself. You will not feel you are ___11___.

There are many ___12___ managers and entertainers who do not like themselves. ___13___, they seem successful, but deep down they are miserable. They know they are contributing very little of real value and all the time they live in fear of ___14___ as cheats. They know they are not earning their wealth. They know they are cheating the company, the ___15___ or society. But they can't fool themselves.

Oral Activities

Activity One

Group Discussion: What does happiness mean to you?

Various people have different perspectives towards happiness.

"Happy is the man who is living by his hobby." (G. Bernard Shaw, British dramatist)

"Happiness lies not in the mere possession of money; it lies in the joy of achievement, in the thrill of creative effort." (Franklin Roosevelt, American president)

"Most folks are about as happy as they make up their minds to be." (Abraham Lincoln, American president)

"The supreme happiness of life is the conviction that we are loved." (Victor Hugo, French novelist)

You may find happiness in the small things or events of life. Happiness may mean a cup of warm tea on a rainy day. Happiness may mean being able to wake up each morning to see the family's smiles. Happiness may mean knowing who and what you are, and having made the most of the positive and the least of the negative in your life.

Unit 6 Happiness

What does happiness mean to you? Discuss in groups and each group should then share the outcome of the discussion to the rest of the class.

Activity Two

Debate: Can money buy happiness?

Can money buy happiness? Different people hold different opinions. Some people regard money as the source of happiness. They hold the opinion that financially richer people tend to be happier. Money can buy enjoyment, comfort and security. However, some people still believe that there is no connection between money and happiness and happiness is not the twin brother of money. Some even view money as the root of all evil. The desire for money may drive people to lie, to steal, to break the law, and so on. Money may ruin life if people overindulge themselves in luxuries.

What is your opinion on this topic? Discuss the question with your classmates and make a debate.

The class will be split into two groups.

Pros: Money can buy happiness.   Cons: Money can't buy happiness.

Writing Practice

Note Writing:

You are supposed to meet your friend Rose this afternoon, but something unexpected prevents you from making it. Write a note to her explaining the reasons and asking whether you could meet her next Wednesday afternoon. Your note should be about 60 words.

Sunday 9:00 AM

Dear Rose,

Yours,
Jack

Paragraph Writing:

People always say "Cheer up! No worries!" and "The most important thing is being happy." to encourage each other. However, what is happiness in your mind? Is happiness equal to fortune, love, health, a most desired profession, or travelling around the world? What shall we do to obtain happiness?

Present your views of happiness in a paragraph in about 120 words.

Unit 7 Dreams

Warm-up Activities

1. Do you always remember your dreams? Share with your classmates a wonderful, scary or weird dream you once had.
2. What is your dream for the future? Have your dreams for your future ever changed?

Text I

Creating Your Dreams

Pre-reading Questions

1. Is there anything we can gain from our dreams?
2. Have you ever used a dream to solve a waking-life problem?

We are such stuff as dreams are made on.

—William Shakespeare, *The Tempest*

1   The most immediate effect of a big dream on a person's life is to seize his or her conscience awareness. Certain dreams are so powerful, so numinous, so incredibly, intensely vivid and realistic that they absolutely force the dreamer to pay attention. Dreamers may not know right away what their experiences mean, and they may never be able to translate their dreams' amazing images and unforgettable sensations into rational language. But at a fundamental level, the simple presence of the dream in the dreamer's consciousness is what matters most. This entrance of the dream into waking-world awareness is itself a kind of creative process, a transformation of the dream from one dimension of reality to

another. All big dreams are driven by an essential desire to create: All big dreams seek an ever greater presence in the dreamer's life, and all big dreams strive to bring new realities into existence. The final stage of interpreting a big dream is doing whatever you can to satisfy this creative energy welling up from within the dream.

2   A great deal of research has been done on the relationship between dreaming and creativity, and the basic findings of this research are fairly easy to summarize. Dreaming appears to be one of the crucial elements in the process of problem solving. This process occurs whenever a person faces a challenge requiring a creative solution, whether it's a challenge involving a personal relationship, an intellectual puzzle, an issue at work, or an attempt at making a piece of art.

3   Researchers have identified this process of dream-inspired problem solving in a wide variety of settings. Artists, of course, make frequent use of the creative power of dreaming—a musician may struggle to play a certain song well and then has a dream that reveals a new technique that dramatically improves the performance of that song. Scientists, too, have found that dream images can disclose new insights into the thorniest difficulties of their work, suggesting new possibilities for their theories, equations, and experiments. Numerous inventors have discovered that some of their strangest dreams have provided breakthrough ideas in designing and building new tools and mechanical devices. In the realm of religion, dreams can be regarded as problem solvers par excellence—people from all over the world have experienced their despair, and creatively reoriented their lives. Perhaps the most commonly experienced form of problem solving through dreams comes in the context of personal relationships—when a person is having serious troubles with a family member or a romantic partner, a special dream will sometimes come that gives the person a creative new way of working through the troubles.

4   The best explanation that researchers can give for the problem-solving power of certain dreams is that dreaming allows for a more flexible and wider

ranging mode of thinking than is ordinary possible in waking consciousness. In dreaming, the mind is looser, more fluid, more playful. Dreaming is a realm of pure freedom, and this liberation from the constraints of external social reality allows the mind to try out the great variety of possible solutions to the given problem. Brainstorming is the word people use when they want to describe this mode of thinking in a waking state. Current research suggests that dreaming is the original form of brainstorming and that, in fact, no attempt by waking consciousness can ever match dreaming for sheer creative energy and dynamism.

5   When learning about these important research findings on dreams and creativity, people sometimes neglect the importance of the testing process. A dream cannot in and of itself solve a waking-life problem; what is always necessary is the willingness of the dreamer to pay conscious attention to the dream, to test its workability, and finally to act on its guidance. It is tempting to think that simply having a powerful dream will turn an ordinary person into a famous artist or a revolutionary scientist, but, for better or for worse, it doesn't work that way. Artists and scientists are able to make use of their dreams in special ways because they have the practical training and the technical skills necessary to do so. Dreams inspire those who are prepared to be inspired and who are able to do the practical work to transform their inspirations into realities.

6   In my view the key finding of current research on this subject is that dreams serve a creative, problem-solving function in all people. Wherever people live, whatever kind of work they do, whatever kind of challenges they face, their dreams offer them a true wellspring of creative possibility. Although there are many wonderful examples of famous people having creative inspirations in their dreams, I believe such examples can actually obscure the most important point here—that nonfamous people, too, have dreams of astonishing creative power. All people have this power within them, a power that can change the way they think, feel and behave in waking life.

(838 words)

Words and Expressions

conscious   /ˈkɒnʃəs/   adj. awake and able to understand what is happening around you 有意识的,有知觉的   consciousness n.

awareness	/əˈweənɪs/	n.	the ability to notice something using your senses 意识
numinous	/ˈnjuːmɪnəs/	adj.	having a mysterious and holy quality; supernatural 超自然的
incredibly	/ɪnˈkredəbli/	adv.	extremely 非常，十分
realistic	/rɪəˈlɪstɪk/	adj.	presenting things as they are in real life 逼真的，栩栩如生的
image	/ˈɪmɪdʒ/	n.	a mental picture of something not real or present 幻象
sensation	/senˈseɪʃən/	n.	the general feeling or expression caused by a particular experience 感觉
rational	/ˈræʃənəl/	adj.	based on reason rather than emotion 理性的
fundamental	/ˌfʌndəˈmentl/	adj.	relating to the most basic and important parts of something 基本的，基础的
transformation	/ˌtrænsfəˈmeɪʃən/	n.	a complete change in someone or something 转换，改变
well	/wel/	vi.	(also well up) to rise from an inner source 涌出，流出
creativity	/ˌkriːeɪˈtɪvɪti/	n.	the ability to use your imagination to produce new ideas, make things, etc. 创造力
fairly	/ˈfeəli/	adv.	more than a little, but much less than very 相当，还，尚
summarize	/ˈsʌməraɪz/	vi/vt.	to make a summary or make a summary of 概述，总结
creative	/kriˈeɪtɪv/	adj.	involving the use of imagination to produce new ideas or things 创造性的
involve	/ɪnˈvɒlv/	vt.	to include or affect 包含，涉及
intellectual	/ˌɪntɪˈlektʃuəl/	adj.	relating to the ability to think and to understand ideas and information 智力的
issue	/ˈɪsjuː/	n.	an important subject that people are arguing about or discussing 重要问题，议题
identify	/aɪˈdentɪfaɪ/	vt.	to recognize something or discover exactly what it is 识别，发现
setting	/ˈsetɪŋ/	n.	a particular place or type of surroundings where something is or takes place 背景，场合
reveal	/rɪˈviːl/	vt.	to make known something that was previously

Unit 7 Dreams

			secret or unknown 揭示,展现
dramatic	/drəˈmætɪk/	adj.	great and sudden 急剧的 **dramatically** adv.急剧地
disclose	/dɪsˈkləʊz/	vt.	to make something known 透露,揭示
insight	/ˈɪnsaɪt/	n.	a sudden clear understanding of something 洞悉,深入了解
thorny	/ˈθɔːnɪ/	adj.	complicated and difficult 棘手的
equation	/ɪˈkweɪʃən/	n.	a statement in mathematics that shows that two amounts or totals are equal 等式
numerous	/ˈnjuːmərəs/	adj.	many 众多的,许多的
mechanical	/mɪˈkænɪkəl/	adj.	using power from an engine or from electricity when working 机械的
device	/dɪˈvaɪs/	n.	a machine or tool that does a special job 装置,器具,设备
realm	/relm/	n.	a general area of knowledge, activity, or thought 领域,范围
par excellence	/ˌpɑːrˈeksəlɑːns/	adj.	the very best of a particular thing 最优秀的,卓越的
orient	/ˈɔːrɪent/	vt.	to learn about and prepare to deal with 使适应,使具备应付能力 **reorient** vt. to orient again in a better way 调整,再适应
romantic	/rəʊˈmæntɪk/	adj.	relating to feelings of love or a loving relationship 浪漫的,爱情的
work through			to deal with problems or unpleasant feelings 应对
mode	/məʊd/	n.	a particular way or style of behaving, living or doing something 模式,方式
fluid	/ˈfluːɪd/	adj.	changeable 不固定的,可变的
constraint	/kənˈstreɪnt/	n.	something that limits or controls what you can do 约束,限制
external	/ɪkˈstɜːnl/	adj.	relating to your environment or situation, rather than to your own qualities, ideas, etc. 外在的,外部的
try out			to test 试验
brainstorming	/ˈbreɪnstɔːmɪŋ/	n.	a method of shared problem solving in which all members of a group spontaneously contribute ideas 集思广益,集体自由讨论以谋求解决办法
current	/ˈkʌrənt/	adj.	happening or existing now 目前的,当前的
sheer	/ʃɪə/	adj.	completely such 十足的,完全的

dynamism	/'daɪnəmɪzəm/	n.	energy and determination to succeed 活力，劲头
neglect	/nɪ'glekt/	vt.	to pay too little attention to 忽视
workable	/'wɜːkəbəl/	adj.	practical and effective 可行的　**workability** n. 可行性
tempting	/'temptɪŋ/	adj.	(of something) making you want to do or have 诱人的
for better or (for) worse			whether it is good or bad 不管还是不好
inspiration	/ˌɪnspə'reɪʃən/	n.	an creative idea that you get suddenly 灵感
wellspring	/'welˌsprɪŋ/	n.	a source 源泉
obscure	/əb'skjʊə/	vt.	to prevent something from being seen or heard properly 遮掩，遮蔽
astonishing	/əs'tɒnɪʃɪŋ/	adj.	so surprising that it is difficult to believe 惊人的

Reading Comprehension

I. Decide which of the following best expresses the author's opinion on dreams.

  A. Dreams can be transformed into waking-world realities.

  B. The creative power of dreams can be possessed by all people.

  C. Dreaming is one of the most important elements in problem solving.

  D. Dreaming provides people more modes of thinking and a greater variety of solutions.

II. Answer the following questions.

  1. What is your understanding of "a big dream"? What is the immediate effect of a big dream on a person's life?
  2. According to the passage, what is the relationship between dreaming and creativity? Explain with examples.
  3. In what ways can people make use of the power of their dreams?
  4. Why do people have stronger problem-solving power in their dreams?
  5. Can a dream itself solve a problem in one's real life? Why or why not?
  6. In the author's opinion, what is the most important function of dreams for ordinary people?

Unit 7　Dreams

III. Judge, according to the text, whether the following statements are true or false. For false statements, write the facts in parentheses.

1. People have to pay attention to their dreams because they are so powerful, divine, vivid, and true to life.
   (　　　　　　　　　　　　　　　　　　　　　　　　　　　　　　)
2. The dream enters into real-world awareness through a creative process which completely changes the dream from one aspect of reality to another.
   (　　　　　　　　　　　　　　　　　　　　　　　　　　　　　　)
3. No matter what challenges may come up at any time, the process of problem solving will occur.
   (　　　　　　　　　　　　　　　　　　　　　　　　　　　　　　)
4. In the religious field, dreams can be considered as the unparalleled problem solvers.
   (　　　　　　　　　　　　　　　　　　　　　　　　　　　　　　)
5. If people have serious troubles in personal relationships, they can always find the best solutions in their dreams.
   (　　　　　　　　　　　　　　　　　　　　　　　　　　　　　　)
6. In dreams, people can have a wider perspective of ideas to solve problems.
   (　　　　　　　　　　　　　　　　　　　　　　　　　　　　　　)
7. A powerful dream can turn an ordinary individual into a famous or great person.
   (　　　　　　　　　　　　　　　　　　　　　　　　　　　　　　)
8. All people, no matter where they live and what they do, are bound to have creative power offered by dreams.
   (　　　　　　　　　　　　　　　　　　　　　　　　　　　　　　)

IV. Paraphrase, use your own words to explain the sentences in the text with the help of the context.

1. (Para. 1) ...they may never be able to translate their dreams' amazing images and unforgettable sensations into rational language.

   _____

   _____

2. (Para. 1) But at a fundamental level, the simple presence of the dream in the dreamer's consciousness is what matters most.

   _____

   _____

3. (Para. 3) Scientists, too, have found that dream images can disclose new insights into the thorniest difficulties of their work, ...

_____

4. (Para. 4) ...dreaming allows for a more flexible and wider ranging mode of thinking than is ordinarily possible in waking consciousness.

_____

5. (Para. 4) ...no attempt by waking consciousness can ever match dreaming for sheer creative energy and dynamism.

_____

6. (Para. 5) Dreams inspire those who are prepared to be inspired and who are able to do the practical work to transform their inspirations into realities.

_____

Vocabulary Exercises

I. **Fill in each blank with one of the two words from each pair and note the difference of meaning between them. Change the form when necessary.**

1. INCREDIBLE   INCREDULOUS

   A. He was too _____ of what other people say, and that was why he was taken in.

   B. The manager thinks it almost _____ that no one noticed these errors.

   C. The view from the top of the mountain is just _____.

   D. Over her shoulder, Ella shot him an _____ look.

2. SENSE   SENSATION

   A. The violence scenes in the film caused a _____.

   B. After finishing the jigsaw, he looked around the room with a _____ of achievement.

   C. One sign of a heart attack is a tingling _____ in your left arm.

D. Sugar gives a _____ of sweetness.
E. Dogs have a very cute _____ of smell.

3. DISCLOSE   REVEAL
A. The witness refused to _____ the identity of the murderer.
B. The curtain opened and _____ the grand prize.
C. The violinist _____ himself as a talented interpreter of classical music.
D. The president _____ the fact that he had been in prison twice before.
E. She _____ her even teeth whenever she smiles.

II. **Fill in the blank in each sentence with a word or phrase taken from the box in its appropriate form.**

insight	rational	fluid	par excellence
well up	divine	external	thorny
act on	seize	identify	for better or (for) worse

1. Work is, _____ , becoming more flexible in recent years.
2. The researchers are arguing over the _____ points in their projects.
3. A loose and _____ style of dancing is popular among young people.
4. Shakespeare is considered to be a playwright, poet and actor _____ .
5. His article gives us a real _____ into the causes of the present economic crisis.
6. When she saw his face, she was _____ by panic.
7. It is impossible to have a _____ conversation with that woman.
8. Volunteers can be easily _____ by their red caps.
9. Only _____ revelation can remedy man's natural alienation from God.
10. The product should be advertised internally and _____ .
11. We sometimes _____ our instinct to make judgments.
12. I felt tears _____ in my eyes while watching the movie.

Translation Exercises

Translate each of the following sentences into English, using the word or phrase given in the brackets.

1. 我们期盼很久的税收制度改革将要实现了,明年将实行新的税收制度。(bring... into)

2. 这些广告攻势对销售额并没有起多大作用,因此公司正在考虑调整他们的销售模式。(have effect on)

3. 在周密计划了两年后,他们开始将祖国统一的梦想转化为行动。(translate... into)

4. 对于守财奴夏洛克来说,亲情和友情并不重要,金钱才是惟一重要的东西。(matter)

5. 得知自己在比赛中获得第一名后,她想起了过去四年辛苦的训练,不禁热泪盈眶。(well up)

6. 最近在伦敦举行的国际商务会谈已经表明,棘手的问题也可以在友好的气氛下讨论。(thorny)

7. 医学上的这一突破表明,男人们的啤酒肚并不完全是因为狂饮啤酒造成的。(breakthrough)

8. 如果你担忧过多或者是个完美主义者,就有可能患上考试焦虑症。(have trouble with)

9. 我认为,如果人们尽可能地少使用私家车的话,空气污染就会减少。(in one's view)

Text II
The Manifest and Latent Meaning of Dreams

> *Pre-reading Questions*
> 1. Do you often remember nightmares or good dreams?
> 2. What is the average number of dreams a person usually has in one night?

1 Sigmund Freud advanced in *The Interpretation of Dreams* the hypothesis that dreams had both an obvious or manifest meaning and a symbolic or latent meaning. The manifest meaning of a dream is simply what appears most obvious as a dream's theme. Freud also used the phrase 'pictorial value' to describe the manifest content of dreams. For example, a college football player told me the following dream: I was coming out of the dorm, and people were just standing around. I started to run into them, knocking into them and knocking them over. Just then an airplane swooped over our heads and started machine-gunning them. I wasn't hit.

2 I think that the obvious or manifest meaning of this dream is easy to interpret. It contains a common theme of hostility or aggression. To come to the conclusion that a 19-year-old football player's dreams contain hostility is not exceptionally helpful. It could be helpful, of course, but Freud and other dream theorists have made the argument that the latent meanings of dreams are far more useful. Freud thought that the latent and symbolic meanings of dreams provided for a much richer interpretation.

3 Freud thought that the manifest meanings of dreams were chosen from our waking daily life. Much of this material might be from the previous waking day, yet frequently there might also be scenes from our childhood. However, Freud believed that no recent waking idea or scene from the past was chosen randomly. He believed that strong unconscious issues were ultimately selected from the myriad waking ideas and old memories. He thought these unconscious issues were still too scary and powerful to be perceived even by the consciousness of the dream state. Thus, the issues became symbolized or hidden by an automatic process of the psyche. For example, I recently had the following dream: I was

outside a metal building whose inside consisted of ugly metal beams. I was remembering in the dream that this building had something to do with the draft and that I had been there 30 years ago. A bad feeling welled up inside as I recalled the memory of having been sent a letter to report for my draft physical during the Vietnam War. I tried to remember whom I was with when I was in this building, and I recalled it was two buddies from high school. I remembered their names in my dream. I kept thinking, once one was inside the building, it was too late to resist. We were herded like cattle through various stations until we came out, and then no resistance was possible. But now the building was unused and just a smelly relic. I stood outside in the sunshine and kept thinking, 30 years ago, the draft was like a holocaust for 18-year-olds.

4   I do not think it is likely that I could pick out my own latent issues in this dream. I could probably figure out something, but I think my own unconscious resistance will prevent me from determining major unconscious themes. However, I present the dream to show how manifest content is not chosen randomly. This dream, whose manifest content was full of anxious themes, appears to remind me of the long-forgotten fears I had of being drafted and sent to Vietnam. Also, it now reminds me of the helplessness I felt. I was only in my second year of college. I wanted to finish my degree. I did not want to be separated from my wife and son, and I did not want to die.

5   No doubt the themes of helplessness and death are common major issues for nearly everyone and are probably impossible to solve. No rationalization is ever fully successful in keeping them at bay, and probably some ego defenses are more successful than others in keeping one's major unconscious issues hidden. However, eventually something in our current daily lives will subtly or unconsciously remind us of our major issues, and invariably we dream about them.

6   The psychotherapist could use both the manifest and latent content of the dream for discussion in psychotherapy. As I stated earlier, I believe that the manifest content is relatively easy to recognize. For example, in my previously related dream, the overt theme appeared to be anxiety. If we depart from Freudian theory briefly, there is some empirical support that suggests that recent waking

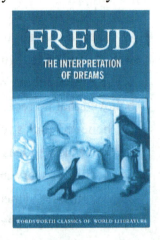

anxieties create anxiety dreams. Thus, a therapist might say, 'Fred, your dream contains some obviously anxious themes. What do these anxious feelings make you think about in your current life?' Here, the therapist will simply use a process of free association to find some current worrisome material in Fred's life. However, remember that I stated that manifest content is not that exciting or compelling? I believe that the therapist could possibly help the patient solve their current worry only to find that a plethora of daily worries hurry to replace that solved one. I think that the therapist will benefit the patient more if the therapist can help the patient solve or even begin to think about the 'original' anxiety or even one of them. I believe, like Freud, that it is early childhood or adolescent issue that triggers the current adult situational anxiety. Because most therapies operate on the principle that awareness, per se, is curative, just having the patient becoming aware that the current anxiety may take the form of an early childhood issue may be helpful, and the therapist does not have to take the form of the responsibility for solving the issue. I trust, like Carl Rogers, a humanistic therapist, that the patient knows best how to solve the problem. If the therapist help the patient to become aware of the old issue and provides an unconditionally positive or safe psychotherapeutic environment, the patient will eventually provide a correct solution.

(968 words)

Reading Comprehension

I. **Answer the following questions with the information you got from the passage.**
   1. What does the football player's dream mean?
   2. In Freud's opinion, what dream is more useful, the manifest one or the latent one? Why?
   3. Where do latent dreams come from?
   4. How does psychotherapist apply dreams for psychotherapy?

II. **Topics for discussion and reflection.**
   1. Try to interpret one of your dreams.
   2. It is said that the more senses you can experience in dreams (colors, smell, etc.), the greater your intelligence is in general. How do you think of it?

Exercises for Integrated Skills

I. Dictation

Listen to the following passage. Altogether the passage will be read to you four times. During the first reading, which will be read at normal speed, listen and try to understand the meaning. For the second and third readings, the passage will be read sentence by sentence, or phrase by phrase, with intervals of 15 to 20 seconds. The last reading will be done at normal speed again and during this time you should check your work. You will then be given 2 minutes to check through your work once more.

II. Cloze

Fill in each blank in the passage below with a word or phrase taken from the box in its appropriate form.

puzzle	take	get away	rare	occur
average	alternate	irritate	rest	psychology
ease	reach	repeat	dry	health

Sleep and Dreams

It's clear that everyone needs to sleep. Most people __1__ think about how and why they sleep, however. We know that if we sleep well, we feel __2__. If we don't sleep enough, we often feel tired and __3__. It seems there are two purposes of sleep: physical rest and emotional or __4__ rest. We need to rest our bodies and our minds. Both are important in order for us to be __5__. Each night we __6__ between two kinds of sleep: active sleep and passive sleep. The passive sleep gives our body the rest needed and prepares us for active sleep, in which dreaming __7__.

Unit 7 Dreams

Throughout the night, people alternate between passive and active sleep. The brain rests, then it becomes active, then dreaming occurs. This cycle __8__ several times throughout the night. During eight hours of sleep, people dream for a total of one and half hours on the __9__ .

No form of thinking is more interesting than dreams. "Brain Wave" machines have shown that dreams last only two to ten seconds. Yet they may tell a story that seems to __10__ hours even days. Some dreams can be explained by feelings of the moment. A __11__ throat might make us dream about the Sahara Desert. The sudden buzzing of a flying thing might become an airplane. Dreams can tell much more about people. Important dreams show our wishes and worries. Sometimes they are so difficult to understand that an expert will feel __12__ , but they may find a struggle to climb up a hill means that we are afraid that we will not __13__ our aims. He may say that our dream about flying without wings means that we are tired of struggling and want to __14__ from it. Dreams of this kind are a normal way to __15__ our worries.

Oral Activities

Dreams play a very important part in our lives. The power of a dream may enable you to achieve your goal, as Langston Hughes said, "Hold fast to dreams for if dreams die, life is a broken winged bird that cannot fly," and David Bower, "Dream the dreams that have never been dreamt."

1. How can you make your dream a reality? Discuss all your dreams in groups and then share them with the class.
2. If you had Aladdin's magic lamp that would allow you three wishes, what wishes would you like to make?

Writing Practice

Note Writing:

You just got the news that Eric, your roommate, has realized his dream of becoming a pop singer. Write a note of congratulation in about 60 words.

April ____

Dear Eric,

Yours,
Henry

Passage Writing:

Dreams
Langston Hughes

Hold fast to dreams
For if dreams die
Life is a broken-winged bird
That can never fly.
Hold fast to dreams
For when dreams go
Life is a barren field
Frozen with snow.

The above is a poem on dreams. Nowadays, some people have dreams of becoming rich while others may dream of flying to the moon. What is your dream? Think about this question and write a 200-word paragraph describing your dreams.

Unit 8 Hobbies

Warm-up Activities

1. Having a hobby is a great way to relax and enjoy your free time. Please make a list of some common hobbies.
2. How might hobbies be different around the world, across China and between people of different ages?
3. Act out some of your favourite hobbies and let your classmates guess what they are.

Text I

Favorite Hobby—Reading

Pre-reading Questions

1. What are the three best books or stories you have ever read? When did you first read them? What are they about?
2. What benefits do you see in reading? How do you think reading helps you in your daily life?

1   Reading is one of the most constructive hobbies a person can have. The difference between ignorance and knowledge is only a book away. Reading stimulates your mind. It makes you think. You can learn to do many other hobbies by reading. It will generate in you new ideas and a more sound understanding of the world and those around you. Almost all great men and women have had a love of reading and a passion for learning.

2	Reading can be a relaxing hobby as well. It is something you can just sit around in your house and do. You can go to the park and read. You can go up into the mountains or out in the field to read alone if you would like. You can get completely lost in reading and forget where you are or what time it is, or how much time has passed while you have been reading. If you do not like reading, do it anyway, until you learn to love it. Read different types of books to see which genre of books are most interesting to you.

3	Reading can fit all personality types, whether you like fiction or non-fiction, action, adventure, drama, humor, whatever it may be, there are books that will fit your tastes. I try to read books as often as I can. I have a personal website now, where I created a book club and can make comments or reviews of the books I read. I think I enjoy every book that I read. Every single one has something to offer, something to learn from it.

4	The more you put into a book, the more you get out of it. You can read a very boring book, but if you read between the lines you can find surprising things that interest you. Think of the deeper meanings of the stories and the lessons the authors are trying to teach, whether you agree with them or not. If you do not agree with them, think to yourself why. Look at the stories of the lives of the people in the books and reflect what you can learn from them. I enjoy reading nonfiction books, but I can enjoy any book that is well written and has deep and insightful truths.

5	Books can make you see the world differently. They can make you understand things more fully and wholly. They can change your paradigm. They will increase your vocabulary, your understanding of life and people, and with this understanding, you will gain more confidence in your social interactions. You will be able to argue your opinions more thoroughly and logically. You will understand the current issues to a greater extent. When you learn to understand others better, you can become more tolerant and respectful of differing opinions. Your opinions will become more logical and solidified. They may change and be molded as they are solidifying from your increase in knowledge.

6 It does not matter what your interests and hobbies are, reading is a good way to start. Reading will enhance your quality of life in every area and facet of your life. Escape the world and get into a book. Live the lives of thousands of others in the books you read. Share their adventures. Learn what they have learned. Find out answers to life's most deep and troubling questions. In books you may find things you were never looking for. You may find yourself. You may find that you have much in common with the characters you are reading about. They can inspire you to overcome obstacles and challenges as they have done. They can assure you that if you fight on you can overcome seemingly impossible challenges. So start your hobby today of reading, or start your hobby by reading. Find hobbies and books at your nearest hobby shop or library.

(643 words)

Words and Expressions

constructive	/kənˈstrʌktɪv/	adj.	useful and helpful, or likely to produce good results 建设性的,有裨益的
ignorance	/ˈɪɡnərəns/	n.	lack of knowledge or information about something 无知
stimulate	/ˈstɪmjʊleɪt/	vt.	to encourage or help an activity to begin or develop further 刺激,促进
generate	/ˈdʒenəreɪt/	vt.	to produce or cause something 使发生,产生
genre	/ˈʒɑːnrə/	n.	a particular type of art, writing, music, etc., which has certain features that all examples of this type share 种类,类型
review	/rɪˈvjuː/	n.	an article in a newspaper or magazine that gives an opinion about a new book, play, film etc. 书评文章,评论
insightful	/ˈɪnsaɪtfəl/	adj.	able to understand or showing that you understand what a situation or person is really like 有洞察力的
paradigm	/ˈpærədaɪm/	n.	a very clear or typical example of something 示例,范例
interaction	/ˌɪntərˈækʃən/	n.	the activity of talking to other people, working together with them, etc. 交际,交往
tolerant	/ˈtɒlərənt/	adj.	allowing people to do, say, or believe what they want

			without criticizing or punishing them 容忍的,宽容的
respectful	/rɪsˈpektfəl/	adj.	feeling or showing respect 恭敬的,尊重人的
differ	/ˈdɪfə/	vi.	to be different from something in some way 不同,相异
solidify	/səˈlɪdɪfaɪ/	vt.	to make an agreement, plan, attitude, etc. more definite and less likely to change 巩固
mold	/məʊld/	vt.	to influence someone so that they will have particular qualities or behave in a particular way 对……产生影响,陶冶
facet	/ˈfæsɪt/	n.	one of several parts of someone's character, a situation, etc. 方面
obstacle	/ˈɒbstəkəl/	n.	something that makes it difficult to achieve something 障碍

Reading Comprehension

I. Decide which of the following best states the author's purpose for writing.

    A. To tell the readers what they can find in books.

    B. To introduce the advantages of reading.

    C. To persuade the readers to start reading as a new hobby.

II. Write down the topic sentence in each paragraph.

    Para. 1 _____

    Para. 2 _____

    Para. 3 _____

    Para. 4 _____

    Para. 5 _____

Unit 8　Hobbies

Para. 6 _____

_____

III. **Answer the following questions orally.**
   1. What is the difference between ignorance and knowledge in the author's opinion? What do you think?
   2. Why is reading a relaxing hobby?
   3. How can reading fit all personality types?
   4. What is the meaning of the sentence, "The more you put into a book, the more you get out of it"?
   5. Do you believe books can make you see the world differently? Explain with examples.

IV. **Paraphrase, use your own words to explain the sentences in the text with the help of the context.**
   1. (Para. 1) It will generate in you new ideas and a more sound understanding of the world and those around you.

   _____
   _____

   2. (Para. 4) You can read a very boring book, but if you read between the lines you can find surprising things that interest you.

   _____
   _____

   3. (Para. 5) They will increase your vocabulary, your understanding of life and people, and with this understanding, you will gain more confidence in your social interactions.

   _____
   _____

   4. (Para. 5) Your opinions will become more logical and solidified. They may change and be molded as they are solidifying from your increase in knowledge.

   _____
   _____

5. **(Para. 6)** They can assure you that if you fight on you can overcome seemingly impossible challenges.

_____

_____

Vocabulary Exercises

I. Fill in each blank with one of the given words and note the difference of meaning between them. Change the form when necessary.

1. ALONE   LONELY

   A. You are not _____ in feeling upset by all that happened, believe me.

   B. —Don't you get _____ being on your own all day long?

   —I was _____ but I didn't feel _____ .

   C. He was reading _____ when the teacher came into the classroom.

2. PASS   PAST

   A. Jim _____ the ketchup (番茄酱) to Susie after putting some on his French fries.

   B. Aunt Mary loves telling us about her exciting _____ as a dancer in Paris.

   C. They kept quiet until the teacher _____ .

   D. Would you mind going _____ my house on your way home?

3. RESPECTFUL   RESPECTABLE   RESPECTED   RESPECTIVE

   A. We all went back to our _____ homes after the movie.

   B. The old gentleman was a very _____ looking person with grey hair and gold spectacles.

   C. The soldiers bowed their heads in _____ silence at the general's funeral.

   D. No one imagined that the apparently _____ businessman was really a criminal.

   E. Mr. Dickson is a highly _____ journalist in my hometown.

4. ASSURE   ENSURE   INSURE   REASSURE

   A. We have _____ our property against any natural disaster.

   B. The ambassador _____ the Prime Minister of his loyalty.

   C. All the necessary measures had been taken to _____ the witness's safety.

   D. They apologized and _____ us that the matter would be dealt with at once.

122

Unit 8 Hobbies

II. Choose a word or phrase that best completes each of the following sentences.

1. I wonder if my long lost neighbor _____ still be alive. Such things _____ and do happen.
   A. may, might   B. can, can   C. must, must   D. can, must
2. Write down what is said or done. Ask a colleague to take a note _____ .
   A. either   B. as well   C. nevertheless   D. yet
3. _____ I did was motivated by fear.
   A. Whenever   B. Whoever   C. Wherever   D. Whatever
4. Inflation might take off again, _____ is elected.
   A. no matter who   B. whatever   C. no matter what   D. whenever
5. _____ was a mystery to me why he never appeared to be especially popular with his classmates.
   A. It   B. He   C. She   D. What

III. Fill in the blank in each sentence with a word or phrase taken from the box in its appropriate form.

constructive	ignorance	generate	interaction
logically	extent	respectful	enhance
have something in common		challenge	

1. At the very beginning, I thought we _____. It's beyond my expectation that we could become friends.
2. The carpet was badly stained, to such a(n) _____ that you couldn't tell its original colour.
3. The new development will _____ 1000 new jobs.
4. I can not figure out why they ridicule this _____ suggestion.
5. We could _____ him and go direct to the chairman, but we'd be skating on very thin ice if we did so.
6. Reducing the gap between rich and poor is one of the main _____ facing the government.
7. This is a(n) _____ museum in which children can actively manipulate the exhibits.
8. She is not herself now. You'd better keep at a _____ distance from her.

9. Those clothes do nothing to _____ her appearance.
10. There's no _____ in spending money on things you don't need.

Translation Exercises

Translate each of the following sentences into English, using the word or phrase given in the brackets.

1. 他每天都浏览因特网上的头条新闻,并且经常对这些新闻发表评论。(make comments)

2. 这本新书的主要贡献在于它对当前形势的分析富有洞察力。(insightful)

3. 他对自己的将来很有信心,认为自己正在走向成功之路。(confidence)

4. 演讲者列举了充分的理由来证明发展经济不能以牺牲环境为代价。(argue)

5. 朋友之间的互相宽容、互相理解是必不可少的。(tolerant)

6. 为了提高公司声誉,他们决定在电视台的黄金时段为公司产品做广告。(enhance)

7. 几次工作面试失败后,他逐渐意识到了自己的缺点。(conscious of)

8. 他们之间毫无共同之处。不但他们使用的语言没有任何联系,而且生活方式也完全不同。(have... in common)

Text II

Discover Why Knitting Is a Great and Timeless Hobby That You Can Benefit from

> *Pre-reading Question*
>
> Do you like knitting? Or would you attempt to learn it? Why or why not?

1   Knitting is a great hobby. Many people enjoy knitting because of its many benefits. Knitting is considered as a form of art. A completed piece of knitting is in fact a piece of art. The knitter gets to feel a great sense of pride and accomplishment in completing such an item. Living in a fast paced society, many people need to do something to release stress and relax. One of the great benefits of knitting is that it is a splendid stress reliever. It helps to free the mind and hence, it is regarded as a wonderful outlet for an overworked brain. It is no wonder that some people use the activity as a retreat in stressful situations. The craft can slow down a hectic life and enable a person to unwind after a hard day's work. In a world filled with mobile phones, computers, televisions and videos, escaping for an hour to knit something soft and warm can be incredibly rejuvenating. There are people who even believe that knitting can actually fuel the creative process in other areas of their lives. They believe that the craft allows the creative part of the brain to work more effectively and find creative solutions to other areas of their lives.

2   Another benefit of knitting is that it is very portable and can be carried along to any place. Unlike other hobbies like weaving or cooking, the craft can easily be thrown into a bag and pulled out anytime it is required. As such, the knitter can bring the craft along and do it during bus or train journeys, air flights or even in traffic jams.

In this way, hours of waiting and travelling are not wasted away as they are used to accomplish something useful.

3   There are various choices of items to knit such as hats, socks, sweaters, jackets, shawls, scarves and pullovers. There are plenty of projects and designs to choose from to suit all levels of knitting expertise, time and budget. Besides, these pieces can be created to beautify homes or serve as special gifts for loved ones. Knitted garments are beautiful and attractive, and many people like them. Presenting them as gifts is always appreciated.

4   Crafts go through phases. Knitting can create long-lasting items. Home accessories that are hand-knitted with love and care often become heirlooms and family treasures. They are always a source of pride and joy. Besides, these invaluable items are inexpensive to make.

5   What is knitting? It is simply the process of forming a fabric by making interlocking loops from a continuous strand of yarn using two or more needles. Knitting is an easy craft to learn. Besides, it only requires simple materials, which are two knitting needles, some string or yarn, and a little instruction. For certain items, there are some accessories needed. For example, if you are knitting a sweater, then you will need some buttons. The choice of buttons has a great impact on a sweater. They can make the difference between an attractive garment and a stunning one.

6   Knitting is a popular craft among young and old. In fact, the pool of knitting enthusiasts keeps growing. Despite the machine age eliminating the need for hand-stitched items, the popularity of knitting still continues. It is evident that many people have experienced its benefits and recognized its worth and wanted to continue using this craft to enhance their lives.

7   If you are interested in starting knitting as a beginner, there are many resources available with step-by-step knitting instructions to enable you to learn doing simple projects. When you have learned the simple projects, you can proceed to do the more complicated ones. After some time, you can try to create more pieces using your own ideas. Instead of following closely the selected knitting pattern, you can add something of your own to make the design unique.

8   Happy knitting!

(678 words)

Unit 8 Hobbies

Reading Comprehension

I. **Answer the following questions with the information you got from the passage.**
   1. What is knitting? Is it easy to learn?
   2. Why is knitting regarded as a form of art?
   3. Why is knitting popular with both young and old? What benefits can people obtain from knitting?

II. **Topics for discussion and reflection.**
   1. Please discuss with your partners whether knitting is a female hobby or not?
   2. What hobby do you think is the most significant in your life?

Exercises for Integrated Skills

I. **Dictation**

   Listen to the following passage. Altogether the passage will be read to you four times. During the first reading, which will be read at normal speed, listen and try to understand the meaning. For the second and third readings, the passage will be read sentence by sentence, or phrase by phrase, with intervals of 15 to 20 seconds. The last reading will be done at normal speed again and during this time you should check your work. You will then be given 2 minutes to check through your work once more.

   _____
   _____
   _____
   _____
   _____

II. **Cloze**

Fill in each blank in the passage below with a word taken from the box in its appropriate form.

comfort	experiment	choose	companion	date
try	wilderness	background	remove	dark
grief	lose	mission	involve	company

Winston Churchill began his interest in painting in his 40s. As First Lord of the Admiralty (海军大臣) in 1915, he was deeply __1__ in a campaign in the Dardanelles that could have shortened the war. But when the __2__ failed, he paid the price. He __3__ from the admiralty.

"I thought he would die of __4__." said his wife. But he took his home to a farm. There, as Churchill later remembered, "The painting saved me!"

Walking in the garden one day, he happened to see his sister-in-law painting with watercolors. He watched her for a few minutes, then borrowed her brush and __5__ his hand.

Churchill soon decided to __6__ with brushes. Glad to see him free from his __7__ days, his wife rushed to buy whatever she could find. He started with the sky and later described how "carefully I mixed a little blue paint on the palette (调色板), and then made a mark as big as a bean on the snow—white board."

At that time, John Lavery—a Churchill neighbor and famous painter— was teaching him in his art. Later, Lavery said of his student: "if he __8__ painting instead of a politician, he would be a great master with the brush."

In painting, Churchill had found a __9__ with whom he was to walk for the greater part of the years that remained to him. After the war, in 1921, the death of his mother was followed later by the __10__ of his lovely daughter, Marigold. Churchill was very sad, and he found the __11__ in his painting. He wrote to his wife: "I went out and painted a beautiful river in the afternoon, light and golden hills in the __12__. But I kept feeling the hurt of Marigold."

Historians have called the ten years after 1929, when the conservative government fell and Winston was out of office, his __13__ years. But during the ten years, he often painted in the South of France. Of the 500 pictures he left, 250 __14__ from 1930 to 1939.

Painting was a joy to Churchill to the end of his life. He had written in his book Painting as a Pastime, "Light and color, peace and hope, will keep them __15__ to the end of the day."

Unit 8 Hobbies

Oral Activities

1. Each person pursues hobbies according to his/her own interests because hobbies enrich his/her life in various ways. Interview your classmates to find out the most popular hobbies among college students and the reasons why students have such hobbies. Organize your findings and present them to the class.
2. Some argue that promotions, job titles, or being invited to the right parties are what they go after all their lives, while hobbies and pastimes are merely "things to pass the time". How far do you agree with the statement?
3. Some hobbyists spend money on a stamp collection (or other kinds of collections) over a long period but complain the collection doesn't sell for twice what they paid for it. Do you think a hobby should be pursued, first and foremost, for pleasure or for profit?

Writing Practice

Note Writing: Ask for a leave

You have got a bad flu and have to see the doctor this morning. Write a note to Mr. Lee, your teacher, to ask for a sick leave.

May ____

Dear Mr. Lee,

Yours,
Marie

Passage Writing: My Favorite Hobby

Different people have different hobbies. For example, some like reading, some like swimming while others like collecting. What is your hobby? Describe your favorite hobby and state the reasons in about 200 words.

Unit 9 Relationships

Warm-up Activities

1. Is getting along with others a natural ability or does it have to be learned? What type of people do you get along with best?
2. Describe what the relationship with your best friend is like. What qualities do you admire most in him/her and what can the two of you do to help the relationship grow?

Text I

Good Coach-Athlete Relationship through Message-Sending Systems

Pre-reading Questions

1. How do you resolve conflicts in interpersonal relationships (between you and your teacher or one of your classmates)?
2. What do you think of the relationship between an athlete and his/her coach?

1   Participation in athletics should be an enjoyable, rewarding, and enriching experience for both athletes and coaches. But occasionally conflicts between coaches and athletes arise. The conflicts must be addressed and resolved immediately so that the benefits of athletic involvement may continue to contribute to the emotional and physical growth of athletes. In developing good athlete-coach relationship, effective communication plays an important part.

2   Good communication is as stimulating as black coffee, and just as hard to

sleep after. The following recommendations will help coaches effectively send messages to their athletes.

3   **Develop your message** Most of us think we know what we want to say; however, coaches often tell us that they have so much to say that they do not know where to start. Or worse yet, they blast their athletes with enough information to last a lifetime. You must determine what you want to communicate, and stick to it. Be careful not to employ hidden agendas (when the stated purpose and the real purpose of the message are not the same). These types of messages may cause mistrust and decrease the communication with the team.

4   Immediate feedback is more effective and meaningful than delayed feedback, so when possible, coaches should deliver their message at the time they observe the behavior. In other words, when a player gives an outstanding effort, tell him or her immediately rather than waiting until another day, by which time the window of opportunity for the message to have an effect may have closed. Of course, feedback needs to be timed so that strong emotions do not interfere with effective sending of the message or with it being heard in the manner intended.

5   **Get in their heads** Communication is enhanced to the extent that coaches understand their athletes; that is, they should know as much as possible about the values, feelings, and unique situations of their athletes and fellow coaches. Coaches who show understanding lead athletes to believe that they care about them and appreciate what they bring to the team. Once athletes feel understood, appreciated, and cared about, communication is enhanced.

6   Seek first to understand, then to be understood. Before you attempt to offer a solution to a problem, give advice or criticism, or tell your side of the story, seek to understand the perspective of the athlete. When you can "get inside the head" of your athlete and understand his or her value system, interests, and goals, you open the door for effective communication and interdependence.

7 **Tell the truth, directly and specifically** Having the courage to tell the truth greatly increases the trustworthiness and subsequent effectiveness of coaches with their teams. Telling the truth requires character, integrity, and a willingness to be open, direct, and specific in communicating. Coaches who "step up to the plate" and "square up" with athletes are respected and revered. They should provide direct communication to athletes so that there can be no doubt about performance expectations. In conflicts situations, coaches must have the courage and skills to confront athletes so that the conflict can be resolved. The key here is to control emotions so that anger and hostility do not disrupt communication. Coaches often avoid this straightforward approach because they assume that athletes know what they expect or they do not want to hurt athletes' feelings. Credibility and trust are on the line here. Athletes have to know that what they hear from coaches is truthful. Those who hint around or work through a third party (e.g., an assistant coach, athletic trainer, or captain) may find their trustworthiness is questioned. Once trust is broken, it is very difficult to restore. Remember, lies have long lives and create clogged internal arteries of communication that lead to active communication grapevines and powerful rumor mills.

8 In addition to openness, being direct and specific are critical components of being honest. Nothing is more frustrating to an athlete than for a coach to say something like, "You need to get your head into the game." While the coach may believe this covers what needs to be done, the vague message provides very limited information to the athlete about the problem or specific tasks to focus on. Something like this is more on the mark: "Focus on the cues the striker gives you. Watch her hips—if they are open, she is going to your left; if closed, to your right." Athletes need adequate and specific information in order to interpret a message correctly.

9 **Using supportive language and empathy** If you want others to listen, build them up rather than tear them down. That means avoiding threats, sarcasm, negative comparisons, and judgmental statements. Using positive, supportive words and gestures will cause your athletes to want to talk and listen to you. If you pause and think before you speak, you can deliver all of your messages, including criticism, in a positive and supportive way.

10 Empathy is the ability to think and feel another person's experience. It is the process of connecting to others' realities in order to understand not only what

they are thinking and feeling but also how they got to this point. Although empathy begins with listening, messages that are empathetic can create powerful, resilient relationships within the team.

11   Coaches can deliver positive and supportive messages by acknowledging their athletes' efforts; unfortunately, they are much more likely to deliver criticism than praise and positive reinforcement. Negative feedback takes its toll over time. Athletes are loyal when they feel appreciated. Sometimes the most effective communication is to express pride in the athletes' effort or thank them for what they bring to the team. So make sure your communication acknowledges individual as well as team efforts, and deliver those messages frequently.

12   Using supportive and positive language also sends the messages that you respect your athletes. Showing respect means treating athletes as human beings with value rather than as expendable entities. As the veteran baseball manager Sparky Anderson said, "Treat everybody as if they're somebody, because they are." Respect does not mean "smiles-at-all-times" coaching. If athletes perform poorly or make bad decisions, do not ignore it or accept it. On the contrary, showing respect means that you hold athletes accountable for their actions. You call them to task and point out the mistake, but never attack them. A rule of thumb is to demand excellence in terms of performance and be supportive of the athlete as a person. When you criticize performances rather than people, interpersonal relationships remain intact and defensiveness is minimized. When you attack an athlete as a person, you create deep animosity that sometimes cannot be repaired.

13   **Watch body language** Coaches need to watch verbal and nonverbal signs that the athletes they communicate with are receiving their messages. Body language is an excellent indicator, and it is also a good idea to check in periodically with questions such as, "How do you understand what I'm saying?" One of the best ways to verify whether a message has been received, however, is to ask athletes to explain what they heard. By putting the message into their own words, they reveal their level of understanding of the message.

14   **Employ "the sandwich approach" when giving criticism** Coaches must analyze performance and provide criticism in a constructive and nonthreatening manner. As we have said before, that means critiquing behavior and coaching the person.

15   One extremely effective approach to delivering constructive criticisms involves what University of Washington psychologist Ron Smith and his colleagues have labeled "the sandwich approach." For example, in this technique, the coach, using the player's name, first begins with a positive statement, such as "Pat, good effort on getting in front of the ball." Next, the coach gives fortune-oriented instructions—he tells her what to do the next time she is in that situation: "When the ball is coming straight toward you, be sure to get your glove all the way down to the ground." Then he follows this instructive feedback with a positive or encouraging statement that describes how things will improve if his message is heard: "If you practice that, you will be able to consistently field balls at a variety of speeds and bounces." An alternative effective strategy is to follow the corrective instruction with a statement that gives general encouragement, such as "Pat, I really appreciate your consistently good attitude." Thus, the "meat" of the sandwich (future-oriented instruction) comes between the "bread slices" (positive and encouraging statements). The positive statement must be genuine and relate to the present situation. This strategy does not dilute constructive advice; instead it increases the likelihood that the message is received properly and that athletes view their interactions with the coach in a positive manner.

16   **Use more "ands" instead of "buts"**   When giving feedback, the use of "but" increases the chance that only half the message will be heard, and it will usually be the negative half. Even a message delivered in a positive manner will be received more negatively if you use "but" instead of "and". Replacing "but" with "and" fosters a clearer understanding of the message and greater motivation to work on the feedback. Why? Using the word "and" tends to result in both messages being heard. For example, "Nice steal, but you need to work on your transition pass." Inserting "and" results in both messages being heard: "I made a nice steal and I need to work on my transition passes." The positive comment serves as a motivation to work on areas that need improvement.

17   While there can be no guarantee that the above recommendations will avoid all the possible conflicts, those measures can lead to more productive relationships and clearer understandings in the future.

(1,620 words)

Words and Expressions

athletics	/æθˈletɪks/	n.	(*AmE*) physical activities such as sports and exercise 运动，体育运动
rewarding	/rɪˈwɔːdɪŋ/	adj.	making you feel happy and satisfied 有益的，值得的
enrich	/ɪnˈrɪtʃ/	vt.	to make fuller, more meaningful, or more rewarding 使充实，使丰富　**enriching** adj. 充实的，丰富的
address	/əˈdres/	vt.	to start trying to solve (a problem) 着手解决，处理
resolve	/rɪˈzɒlv/	vt.	to find a satisfactory way of dealing with a problem or difficulty 解决
involvement	/ɪnˈvɒlvmənt/	n.	the act of taking part in an activity or event 参与
recommendation	/ˌrekəmenˈdeɪʃn/	n.	official advice given to someone, especially about what to do 建议，劝告
blast	/blɑːst/	vt.	to criticize very strongly 严厉批评
agenda	/əˈdʒendə/	n.	a list of problems or subjects to be dealt with 议题，待办事项
feedback	/ˈfiːdbæk/	n.	advice, criticism, etc. about how successful or useful something is 反馈，反馈意见
interfere	/ˌɪntəˈfɪə/	vi.	to deliberately get involved in a situation where you are not wanted or needed 介入，干涉　**interfere with** 妨碍，扰乱
criticism	/ˈkrɪtɪsɪzəm/	n.	remarks that say what you think is bad about someone or something 批评，批判
perspective	/pəˈspektɪv/	n.	a particular way of thinking about something, especially one which is influenced by your beliefs or experiences 思想方法，视角
trustworthy	/ˈtrʌstˌwɜːði/	adj.	can be trusted and depended on 可信赖的，值得信赖的　**trustworthiness** n. 信赖
subsequent	/ˈsʌbsɪkwənt/	adj.	happening or coming after something else 随后的，后来的
integrity	/ɪnˈtegrɪti/	n.	the quality of being honest and firm in your moral principles 正直

step up to the plate			to take responsibility for doing something 开始行动
square up			to prepare to confront (a problem or a person) 正视，勇敢面对
revere	/rɪˈvɪə/	vt.	to respect and admire greatly 尊敬，敬慕
confront	/kənˈfrʌnt/	vt.	to face someone and be ready to fight or argue 勇敢地面对，与……相对抗
hostility	/hɒˈstɪlɪtɪ/	n.	unfriendly or aggressive behaviour towards people or ideas 敌对，敌意
disrupt	/dɪsˈrʌpt/	vt.	to prevent something from continuing or operating in a normal way by causing problems 使中断，扰乱
credibility	/ˌkredɪˈbɪlɪtɪ/	n.	the quality of deserving to be believed and trusted 信用，可靠性
be on the line			(of something important) to be at risk 不稳定的，有被破坏或失去的风险的
truthful	/ˈtruːθfəl/	adj.	(of someone) usually not telling lies 说实话的
hint	/hɪnt/	vi.	to suggest something in an indirect way 暗示
restore	/rɪˈstɔː/	vt.	to make something return to its former state or condition 恢复，重建
clog	/klɒg/	vt.	to block something or become blocked 阻塞，堵塞 **clogged** adj. 堵塞的
internal	/ɪnˈtɜːnl/	adj.	inside your body 体内的
artery	/ˈɑːtərɪ/	n.	one of the tubes that carries blood from your heart to the rest of your body 动脉
grapevine	/ˈgreɪpvaɪn/	n.	the informal transmission of information, gossip, or rumor from person to person 传言，小道消息
rumor	/ˈruːmə/	n.	(*AmE*, **rumour** *BrE*) information or a story that is passed from one person to another and which may or may not be true 谣言，传闻
rumor mill			a group of people who discuss something and pass rumors to each other 相互传播小道消息的小团体
critical	/ˈkrɪtɪkəl/	adj.	extremely important 关键的，极其重要的
frustrating	/frʌˈstreɪtɪŋ/	adj.	making you feel annoyed, upset, or impatient

Unit 9 Relationships

			because you cannot do what you want to do 令人沮丧的,令人懊恼的
on the mark			accurate or correct 正确的,切题的
cue	/kjuː/	n.	an action or event that is a signal for something else to happen 提示,暗示
striker	/ˈstraɪkə/	n.	a player in football whose main job is to score goals (足球队中的)前锋
hip	/hɪp/	n.	one of the two parts on each side of your body between the top of your leg and your waist 髋,髋部
empathy	/ˈempəθɪ/	n.	the ability to understand other people's feelings and problems 同感,同情,共鸣 **empathetic** *adj.* 同情的;有同感的
sarcasm	/ˈsɑːkæzəm/	n.	speech or writing which actually means the opposite of what it seems to say, usually intended to mock or insult someone 讽刺,嘲笑,挖苦
negative	/ˈnegətɪv/	adj.	harmful, unpleasant, or not wanted 负面的,有害的
judgmental	/dʒʌdʒˈmentəl/	adj.	criticizing people very quickly 动辄批评人的,妄下判断的
resilient	/rɪˈzɪlɪənt/	adj.	strong and not easily damaged by being pulled, pressed, etc. 有弹性的,不易受损的
reinforcement	/ˌriːɪnˈfɔːsmənt/	n.	the process of making something stronger 加强,加固
take its/a heavy toll			have a very bad effect or cause a lot of suffering 造成重大损失或伤害
loyal	/ˈlɔɪəl/	adj.	always supporting your friends, principles, country, etc. 忠诚的
expendable	/ɪkˈspendəbəl/	adj.	not needed enough to be kept or saved 不值得保留的;可牺牲的
entity	/ˈentɪtɪ/	n.	something that exists as a single and complete unit 独立存在体,实体
veteran	/ˈvetərən/	n.	someone who has had a lot of experience in a particular activity 有经验的人,老手
accountable	/əˈkaʊntəbəl/	adj.	responsible for the effects of your actions and

			willing to explain or be criticized for them 应负责任的,有解释义务的
call sb to task			to criticize someone 批评,指责
rule of thumb			a useful principle having wide application but not intended to be strictly accurate or reliable in every situation 经验法则
in terms of			only in relation to that fact or event 在……方面,就……而言
criticize	/ˈkrɪtɪsaɪz/	vt.	to express your disapproval of someone or something, or to talk about their faults 批评,责备
intact	/ɪnˈtækt/	adj.	not broken, damaged, or spoiled 完整无损的
defensive	/dɪˈfensɪv/	adj.	behaving in a way that shows you think someone is criticizing you even if they are not 防御的,自我保护的 **defensiveness** n. 防御
minimize	/ˈmɪnɪmaɪz/	vt.	to reduce something that is difficult, dangerous, or unpleasant to the smallest possible amount or degree 使减至最小,使降到最低
animosity	/ˌænɪˈmɒsɪti/	n.	strong dislike or hatred 敌意,仇恨,憎恶
verbal	/ˈvɜːbəl/	adj.	relating to words or using words 言语的,言词的
indicator	/ˈɪndɪkeɪtə/	n.	something that can be regarded as a sign of something else 指示物,信号
periodic	/ˌpɪərɪˈɒdɪk/	adj.	happening a number of times, usually at regular times 间歇性的,周期的,定期的 **periodically** adv. 间歇性的,周期地,定期地
verify	/ˈverɪfaɪ/	vt.	to discover whether something is correct or true 核实,查证
threatening	/ˈθretənɪŋ/	adj.	making you feel that you will be harmed 威胁的,恐吓的 **nonthreatening** adj. 不具威胁性的
critique	/krɪˈtiːk/	vt.	to say how good or bad a book, play, painting, or set of ideas is 评论,评判
field	/fiːld/	vt.	(in cricket or baseball) to stop a ball after it has been hit (板球或棒球运动中)接球
bounce	/baʊns/	n.	the action of moving upwards from a surface 反弹,弹起
corrective	/kəˈrektɪv/	adj.	intended to make something right or better again 纠正的,矫正的
genuine	/ˈdʒenjuɪn/	adj.	(of emotions) real and not pretended 真实的,真挚的

Unit 9 Relationships

dilute	/daɪˈluːt/	vt.	to make a quality, belief, etc. weaker or less effective 冲淡, 削弱
likelihood	/ˈlaɪklɪhʊd/	n.	the degree to which something can reasonably be expected to happen 可能性
guarantee	/ˌɡærənˈtiː/	vt.	to promise to do something or to promise that something will happen 保证, 担保

Reading Comprehension

I. Write down the sentence or the key words that best sum up the main idea in each paragraph.

Part I Introduction (Paras. 1–2)	
Part II Main body (Paras. 3–16)	Recommendations for enhancing good athlete-coach relationship. 1. (Para.) _____ 2. (Para.) _____ 3. (Para.) _____ 4. (Para.) _____ 5. (Para.) _____ 6. (Para.) _____ 7. (Para.) _____ 8. (Para.) _____
Part III Conclusion (Para. 17)	Prospect of adopting those recommendations.

139

II. **Answer the following questions.**
   1. What are the problems coaches face when delivering messages?
   2. Why is showing understanding important to enhance communication?
   3. What does the author mean by saying "step up to the plate" and "square up"?
   4. How can the coach-athlete relationship be developed through supportive and positive language?
   5. Explain "the sandwich approach" with examples.

III. **Judge, according to the text, whether the following statements are true or false. For false statements, write the facts in parentheses.**
   1. If conflicts between coaches and athletes cannot be solved as soon as possible, they will harm the emotional and physical growth of the athletes.
      (   )
   2. Coaches often don't know what to say to their athletes, and their criticisms could last a lifetime.
      (   )
   3. Coaches should give immediate feedback the moment a player gives a good or bad performance.
      (   )
   4. When athletes feel understood, chances are that they will show understanding to their coaches.
      (   )
   5. Athletes will doubt their coaches' credibility if coaches don't communicate with them directly.
      (   )
   6. To use supportive language, coaches should pause and carefully take the time to think for a while before they talk to their athletes.
      (   )
   7. If athletes perform poorly, coaches should not get angry but give them feedback or suggestions with smiles.
      (   )
   8. When adopting "the sandwich approach", coaches should use positive statements that are sincere and that relate to the present situation.
      (   )

Unit 9 Relationships

IV. **Paraphrase, use your own words to explain the sentences in the text with the help of the context.**

1. (Para. 2) Good communication is as stimulating as black coffee, and just as hard to sleep after.

2. (Para. 4) ... the window of opportunity for the message to have an effect may have closed.

3. (Para. 7) ...lies have long lives and create clogged internal arteries of communication that lead to active communication grapevines and powerful rumor mills.

4. (Para. 9) If you want others to listen, build them up rather than tear them down.

5. (Para. 11) Negative feedback takes its toll over time.

6. (Para. 12) A rule of thumb is to demand excellence in terms of performance and be supportive of the athlete as a person.

7. (Para. 15) This strategy does not dilute constructive advice; instead it increases the likelihood that the message is received properly...

Vocabulary Exercises

I. Choose a word or phrase that best completes each of the following sentences.

1. Slavery was _____ in Canada in 1833, and Canadian authorities encouraged the slaves, who escaped from America, to settle on its vast virgin land.
   A. diluted   B. dissipated   C. abolished   D. resigned

2. The challenge is not one of expansion. _____, the rapid growth in enrollment over the last 40 years has come to an end.
   A. As a result   B. By all means   C. In contrast   D. On the contrary

3. These policies _____ many elderly and disabled people suffering hardship.
   A. made   B. contributed to   C. resulted in   D. led in

4. Mobile phones are proved to _____ with flight instruments and have a negative effect on flight safety.
   A. interfere   B. disturb   C. interrupt   D. trouble

5. A lot of the old houses have been _____ to make way for new buildings.
   A. torn apart   B. torn down   C. torn away   D. torn up

6. Her tragic death should serve _____ a warning to other young people.
   A. as   B. for   C. up   D. out

7. The National Guard was called in to _____ peace in this area.
   A. rebuild   B. regain   C. restore   D. repair

8. There seems to be no solution _____ the problem.
   A. for   B. to   C. of   D. on

II. Fill in the blank in each sentence with a word taken from the box in its appropriate form.

enrich	disrupt	credibility	clogged
enhance	empathy	resilient	animosity
verify	revere		

1. A computer program will be used to _____ that the system is working.
2. That textile factory proved remarkably _____ during the recession.

Unit 9 Relationships

3. He was unable to give a _____ explanation for his behavior.
4. Reading and travel can greatly _____ your life.
5. Over many years, the pipes _____ with rust.
6. Passing the certification test should _____ your chances of getting the post.
7. After the famous war, he was _____ as a national hero.
8. According to the scientist, climate change caused by global warming could _____ the agricultural economy.
9. As a leader, Mr. Brown had great _____ with people.
10. She felt a certain amount of _____ towards her boss.

Translation Exercises

Translate each of the following sentences into English, using the word or phrase given in the brackets.

1. 工会严厉批评他执政后未能减少失业人数，这使得他对解决目前复杂的就业形势失去了信心。(blast)

2. 当他孤身一人在国外创业，事业处于低谷的时候，妻子适时的鼓励与支持是他最大的精神支柱。(time)

3. 社会暴力已经发展到了当地居民不敢在晚上出门的地步。(to the extent that)

4. 他终于明白了自己受观众攻击的真正原因是有些娱乐新闻记者千方百计诽谤他。(get into one's head)

5. 比赛前，教练总是表扬我们，以使我们有足够的信心去打败强大的对手。(build up)

6. 他的失职使整个工程延期了一个月，为此领导非常严厉地批评了他，并要他保证以后准时完成自己的任务。(tear down)

143

7. 如果你没有迅速地把问题的关键点说明白,听者会感到无所适从,并且很难集中精力听接下来的内容。(get to the point)

8. 长时间的超负荷户外作业给他的胃造成了严重的伤害,使他经常呕吐并遭受剧烈的胃疼。(take its toll)

9. 这些做决策的人并不认为自己应该对普通老百姓的经济损失负责。(hold accountable for)

10. 汶川大地震发生后,科学家们一直在严密监测这个区域可能会再次发生的余震;医生们也在密切关注着地震中伤员的病情变化。(watch for)

Text II

The Story of My Life
By Helen Keller

Pre-reading Questions

1. What are some of the qualities that make a super teacher?
2. Do you have a positive relationship with most of your teachers? How do you establish and develop it?

1   The most important day I remember in all my life is the one on which my teacher, Anne Mansfield Sullivan, came to me. I am filled with wonder when I consider the immeasurable contrasts between the two lives which it connects. It was the third of March, 1887, three months before I was seven years old. On the afternoon of that eventful

day, I stood on the porch, dumb, expectant. I guessed vaguely from my mother's signs and from the hurrying to and fro in the house that something unusual was about to happen, so I went to the door and waited on the steps. The afternoon sun penetrated the mass of honeysuckle that covered the porch, and fell on my upturned face. My fingers lingered almost unconsciously on the familiar leaves and blossoms which had just come forth to greet the sweet southern spring. I did not know what the future held of marvel or surprise for me. Anger and bitterness had preyed upon me continually for weeks and a deep languor had succeeded this passionate struggle.

Have you ever been at sea in a dense fog, when it seemed as if a tangible white darkness shut you in, and the great ship, tense and anxious, groped her way toward the shore with plummet and sounding-line, and you waited with beating heart for something to happen? I was like that ship before my education began, only I was without compass or sounding-line, and had no way of knowing how near the harbour was. "Light! Give me light!" was the wordless cry of my soul, and the light of love shone on me in that very hour.

I felt approaching footsteps, I stretched out my hand as I supposed to be my mother. Someone took it, and I was caught up and held close in the arms of her who had come to reveal all things to me, and, more than all things else, to love me. The morning after my teacher came she led me into her room and gave me a doll. The little blind children at the Perkins Institution had sent it and Laura Bridgman had dressed it; but I did not know this until afterward. When I had played with it a little while, Miss Sullivan slowly spelled into my hand the word "d-o-l-l." I was at once interested in this finger play and tried to imitate it. When I finally succeeded in making the letters correctly I was flushed with childish pleasure and pride. Running downstairs to my mother I held up my hand and made the letters for doll. I did not know that I was spelling a word or even that words existed; I was simply making my fingers go in monkey-like imitation. In the days that followed I learned to spell in this uncomprehending way a great many words, among them *pin, hat, cup* and a few verbs like *sit, stand* and *walk*. But my teacher had been with me several weeks before I understood that everything has a name.

One day, while I was playing with my new doll, Miss Sullivan put my big rag doll into my lap also, spelled "d-o-l-l" and tried to make me understand that "d-o-l-l" applied to both. Earlier in the day we had had a tussle over the words "m-u-g" and "w-a-t-e-r." Miss Sullivan had tried to impress it upon me that "m-u-g" is mug and that "w-a-t-e-r" is water, but I persisted in confounding the two. In despair she had dropped the subject for the time, only to renew it at the first opportunity. I became impatient at her repeated attempts and, seizing the new doll, I dashed it upon the floor. I was keenly delighted when I felt the fragments of the broken doll at my feet. Neither sorrow nor regret followed my passionate outburst. I had not loved the doll. In the still, dark world in which I lived there was no strong sentiment or tenderness. I felt my teacher sweep the fragments to one side of the hearth, and I had a sense of satisfaction that the cause of my discomfort was removed. She brought me my hat, and I knew I was going out into the warm sunshine. This thought, if a wordless sensation may be called a thought, made me hop and skip with pleasure.

5   We walked down the path to the well-house, attracted by the fragrance of the honeysuckle with which it was covered. Someone was drawing water and my teacher placed my hand under the spout. As the cool stream gushed over one hand she spelled into the other the word water, first slowly, then rapidly. I stood still, my whole attention fixed upon the motions of her fingers. Suddenly I felt a misty consciousness as of something forgotten—a thrill of returning thought; and somehow the mystery of language was revealed to me. I knew then that "w-a-t-e-r" meant the wonderful cool something that was flowing over my hand. That living word awakened my soul, gave it light, hope, joy, set it free! There were barriers still, it is true, but barriers that could in time be swept away.

6   I left the well-house eager to learn. Everything had a name, and each name gave birth to a new thought. As we returned to the house every object which I touched seemed to quiver with life. That was because I saw everything with the strange, new sight that had come to me. On entering the door I remembered the doll I had broken. I felt my way to the hearth and picked up the pieces. I tried vainly to put them together. Then my eyes filled with tears; for I realized what I had done, and for the first time I felt repentance and sorrow.

7   I learned a great many new words that day. I do not remember what they all were; but I do know that *mother, father, sister, teacher* were among them—words that were to make the world blossom for me, "like Aaron's rod, with flowers." It would have been difficult to find a happier child than I was as I lay

in my crib at the close of that eventful day and lived over the joys it had brought me, and for the first time longed for a new day to come.

(1,060 words)

Reading Comprehension

I. Answer the following questions with the information taken from the passage.
1. What were the immeasurable contrasts before and after Miss Sullivan, the teacher, arrived?
2. In what ways was Helen Keller "like the ship in a dense fog" before her education began?
3. How did Helen Keller feel after she dashed the doll upon the floor? Why did she have such an unusual reaction?
4. When did Helen Keller feel regret and sorrow for the first time? What made her change?

II. Topics for discussion and reflection
1. "The quality of teacher-student relationships is the keystone for all other aspects of classroom management." Do you agree with this? Why or why not?
2. Discuss with your classmates the most effective solutions to major teacher-student relationship problems.

Exercises for Integrated Skills

I. Dictation

Listen to the following passage. Altogether the passage will be read to you four times. During the first reading, which will be read at normal speed, listen and try to understand the meaning. For the second and third readings, the passage will be read sentence by sentence, or phrase by phrase, with intervals of 15 to 20 seconds. The last reading will be done at normal speed again and during this time you should check your work. You will then be given 2 minutes to check through your work once more.

II. Cloze

Fill in each blank in the passage below with a word or phrase taken from the box in its appropriate form.

attractive	security	beneficial	excessive
hide away	establish	decline	absent
adjust	unexpected	private	length
delicate	sense	shift	

"There is a senseless notion that children grow up and leave home when they're 18, and the truth is far from that," says sociologist Larry Bumpass of the University of Wisconsin. Today, __1__ numbers of young adults are living with their parents. "There is a major __2__ in the middle class," declares sociologist Allan Schnaiberg of Northwestern University, whose son, 19, moved back in after an __3__ of eight months.

Analysts cite a variety of reasons for this return to the nest. The marriage age is rising, a condition that makes home and its pleasantness particularly __4__ to young people. A high divorce rate and a __5__ remarriage rate are sending economically pressed and emotionally hurt survivors back to parental shelters. For some, the expense of an away-from-home college education has become so __6__ great that many students now attend local schools.

Living at home, says Knighton, a school teacher, continues to give her __7__ and moral support. Her mother agreed, "It's ridiculous for the kids to pay all that money for rent. It makes __8__ for kids to stay at home." But sharing the family home requires __9__ for all. There are the hassles (争吵) over bathrooms, telephones and __10__. Some families, however, manage the __11__ balancing act. But for others, it proves too difficult. Michelle Del Turco, 24, has been home three times—and left three times.

Unit 9　Relationships

"What I considered a social drink, my dad considered an alcohol problem," she explains. "He never liked anyone I dated, so I either had to __12__ or meet them at friends' home."

Just how long should adult children live with their parents before moving on? Most psychologists feel __13__ homecomings are a mistake. Children, struggling to __14__ separate identities, can end up with "a sense of inadequacy, defeat and failure." And aging parents, who should be enjoying some financial and personal freedom, find themselves stuck with responsibilities. Many agree that brief visits, however, can work __15__ .

Oral Activities

Work in groups and discuss the following questions.

1. Have you ever encountered any family relationship problems? What strategies have you employed to tackle the problems?   What is a good parent-child relationship in your point of view?
2. How do you keep a good relationship with your friends and people around you?
3. The term "guanxi", which literally means relationship, is a popular concept in Chinese society. It emphasizes the value of the personal connection to a decision-maker. Even some Westerners feel that "guanxi" plays a very important role in doing business in China.   How do you understand this social phenomenon? Do you agree that "guanxi" plays a significant role in people's social activities? Does the value of "guanxi" steadily increase or decrease? Present your perspective to the class.

Writing Practice

Note Writing: Thank-you note

You received a wonderful birthday present from your friend, Michael. Write him a thank-you note to express your gratitude. Write the note in about 60 words.

Michael,

June

Yours,
Helen

Passage Writing:

We are not alone in this world: unavoidably, every one of us is involved in relationships with others, such as family, colleagues, classmates or even animals. What is your view towards relationships between people or between people and animals? Choose one of the following topics and express your ideas in about 200 words.

1. Many people have a close relationship with their pets. These people treat their birds, cats, or other animals as members of their family. In your opinion, are such relationships healthy? Why or why not?
2. What is considered a good, healthy parent-child relationship?

Unit 10 Festival

Warm-up Activities

1. What festivals are widely celebrated in the world and what are particular to your country?
2. Describe some activities which usually take place at one important festival in your hometown (gifts/meals/decorations/music...). Compare how people celebrate it now with how people may have celebrated it in the past.
3. The results of a survey conducted by the Chinese Society Survey Bureau show that Christmas is becoming more popular in China, with the Christmas atmosphere no less intense than that in New Year and Spring Festival. Can you explore reasons why the Chinese public is becoming more conscious about the significance of Christmas, and more and more people are beginning to participate and immerse themselves in the spirit of Christmas celebrations? What are your attitudes toward this phenomenon?

Text I

The 4th of July—a Day of Rejoicing

Pre-reading Questions

1. How do people usually celebrate the national birthday in your country? Are there any patriotic activities you often participate in on that day? What are they?

> 2. Can you name some important people of the American Civil War? What are their contributions?

1   The 4th of July is the most important holiday in the USA, for it commemorates that famous day in 1776 when the Americans declared their independence. Congress made the declaration in Philadelphia, and that night in the city there were joyful celebrations which soon became nationwide. Ever since, the 4th of July has been marked in the American calendar as Independence Day, and there are parades and festivities of all kinds.

2   The basic cause of the Americans' struggle for independence against the mother country, England, was too much interference and intolerance from London and very little understanding of American problems and pride. Most galling to the Americans was the assumption by the English Government and the King that they had a right to tax their subjects overseas without their consent and without giving them anything in return.

3   The American Revolution (1775—1783) is regarded by military historians as a war Britain should never have lost. Many colonists were half-hearted about the conflict. After all, they were originally Englishmen and they had no wish to kill their cousins. There were also many loyalists, some of whom fled to Canada, while others joined British regiments in America.

4   The British, too, were divided. It was a war which inspired no patriotism. In the British Parliament there was fierce opposition to the war from a powerful minority, led by Edmund Burke, the great orator. Burke told the House of Commons that he was not interested in what the Law told him he could do, but in what "humanity, reason and justice" told him he should do. Thomas Jefferson, one of the greatest rebel leaders, said: "We might have been a free and great people together." But the British government of that time was obstinate and stupid, and King George III had such an influence on affairs that it has been called "the King's War."

5   As for the troops which the government sent to fight the rebels, they were unenthusiastic and incompetent, especially their leaders. In any case, large numbers of them were German mercenaries, whom the Americans learned to hate. Neither the British nor German troops had been taught to fight the sort of war

the rebels waged against them. They had been taught only to fight set battles. They were bewildered and helpless against the American sharp-shooters who ambushed them in the thick forests.

6   The Americans, to begin with, had no army. In fact, it is quite possible that but for the extraordinary faith and leadership of George Washington, the revolution might have come to nothing. He built an army which remained loyal to him until the end, despite terrible hardships. He also held together the colonies of New England and all the other very different colonies which stretched as far as Georgia in the South. There was no connecting road. The only safe way of traveling from north to south was by sea.

7   George Washington had been an officer in the British Army which fought and defeated the French in the wilderness of Canada twenty years earlier. His experience of this war had opened up to him visions of an exciting future for his country. He was a true frontiersman. He had seen lands which he knew would make an independent America a mighty nation. He was given valuable support by the two great patriots, Thomas Jefferson and Benjamin Franklin. It was Franklin who helped persuade the French to come into the war against the British. They did not need much persuading, for they longed to recover their lost colonies.

8   In 1781 a British army commanded by an exceptionally incompetent general, Lord Cornwallis, surrendered to the Americans at Yorktown, Virginia, and the war was over. Not long afterward, the 13 colonies became states and joined together in a Union.

9   The effect of the American Revolution was far-reaching. *The Declaration of Independence* drawn up by Thomas Jefferson is one of the most important documents ever published, and it dropped like a bombshell on the western world. Here are the two sentences which shook the ruling classes of Europe: "We hold these truths to be self-evident, that all men are created equal, that they are endowed by their Creator with certain unalienable

rights, that among these are life, liberty and the pursuit of happiness." The second sentence was even more disturbing to them: "That to secure these rights, governments are instituted among men, *deriving* their just powers from the consent of the governed."

(803 words)

Words and Expressions

rejoice	/rɪˈdʒɔɪs/	vi.	to feel very happy because something good has happened 欣喜, 高兴 **rejoicing** *n.* 欣喜, 高兴
commemorate	/kəˈmeməreɪt/	vt.	to do something to show you remember an important person or event in the past with respect 纪念
parade	/pəˈreɪd/	n.	a line of people or vehicles that moves through a public place as a way of celebrating an occasion 游行
interfere	/ˌɪntəˈfɪə/	vi.	to try to control or become involved in a situation, in a way that is annoying 干涉, 干预 **interference** *n.* 干涉, 干预
intolerant	/ɪnˈtɒlərənt/	adj.	not willing to accept ways of thinking and behaving that are different from your own 不容忍的, 偏执的 **intolerance** *n.* 不容忍, 偏执
galling	/ˈɡɔːlɪŋ/	adj.	making you feel upset and angry because of something that is unfair, annoying 令人生气的, 使人恼火的
consent	/kənˈsent/	n.	permission for someone to do something 赞成, 同意
half-hearted	/ˌhɑːf ˈhɑːtɪd/	adj.	done without much effort and without much interest in the result 半心半意的, 不认真的
regiment	/ˈredʒɪmənt/	n.	a large group of soldiers (骑兵或炮兵)团
patriotic	/ˌpætrɪˈɒtɪk/	adj.	having or expressing a great love of your country 爱国的 **patriotism** *n.* 爱国主义, 爱国精神, 爱国心
Parliament	/ˈpɑːləmənt/	n.	the main law-making institution in the UK, which consists of the HOUSE OF COMMONS and the

			HOUSE OF LORDS 议会（由上议院和下议院组成）
orator	/ˈɒrətə/	n.	someone who is good at making speeches and persuading people 演说者，雄辩家
humanity	/hjuːˈmænɪtɪ/	n.	the state of being human rather than an animal or machine 人性
rebel	/ˈrebəl/	n.	someone who opposes or fights against people in authority 反叛者，反抗者
obstinate	/ˈɒbstɪnɪt/	adj.	not willing to change your ideas or behavior although you are wrong 固执的，顽固的
enthusiastic	/ɪnˌθjuːzɪˈæstɪk/	adj.	feeling or showing a lot of interest and excitement about something 热情的，热心的 **unenthusiastic** *adj.* 不热情的，不热心的
competent	/ˈkɒmpɪtənt/	adj.	having enough skill or knowledge to do something to a satisfactory standard 有能力的，能胜任的 **incompetent** *adj.* 没有能力的，不能胜任的
mercenary	/ˈmɜːsənərɪ/	n.	a soldier who fights for any country or organization who pays him 雇佣兵
bewildered	/bɪˈwɪldəd/	adj.	very confused and not sure what to do 迷惑的
ambush	/ˈæmbuʃ/	vt.	to attack a person or vehicle after hiding somewhere and waiting for them to arrive 埋伏，伏击
frontiersman	/ˈfrʌntɪəzmən/	n.	a man who lived on the American frontier, especially in the 19th century 边境居民
surrender	/səˈrendə/	vi.	to stop fighting and admit that you have been beaten 投降
endow	/ɪnˈdaʊ/	vt.	to make someone or something have a particular quality, or to believe that they have it 赋予
unalienable	/ˌʌnˈeɪljənəbl/	adj.	unable to be removed 不可转让的
derive	/dɪˈraɪv/	vt.	to get or obtain something from something else 取得，得到

Reading Comprehension

I. **Write down the main idea(s) for each part.**

    1. Paragraph 1 _____

    2. Paragraphs 2–8 _____

      2a. Paragraphs 2 _____

      2b. Paragraphs 3–5 _____

      2c. Paragraphs 6–7 _____

      2d. Paragraph 8 _____

    3. Paragraph 9 _____

II. Answer the following questions orally.

1. Why is the 4th of July the most important holiday in the USA?
2. What caused the American Revolution?
3. What advantages did Britain and America have over each other respectively?
4. Who helped persuade the French to fight against the British? What else do you know about him?
5. What changes came about as a result of the American Revolution?

III. Judge, according to the text, whether the following statements are true or false. For false statements, write the facts in parentheses.

1. There was a unanimous agreement in the British Parliament on the way the war was being handled.
   (   )
2. It was George Washington who built an army and led them to defeat the British army.
   (   )
3. King George III greatly influenced the war.
   (   )
4. The Americans won the war because they got help from the French.
   (   )
5. *The Declaration of Independence* was drafted by Benjamin Franklin.
   (   )

IV. Paraphrase, use your own words to explain the sentences in the text with the help of the context.

1. (Para. 2) Most galling to the Americans was the assumption by the English Government and the King that they had a right to tax their subjects overseas

without their consent and without giving them anything in return.

2. (Para. 3) Many colonists were half-hearted about the conflict.

3. (Para. 6) In fact, it is quite possible that but for the extraordinary faith and leadership of George Washington, the revolution might have come to nothing.

4. (Para. 9) We hold these truths to be self-evident, that all men are created equal, that they are endowed by their Creator with certain unalienable rights, that among these are life, liberty and the pursuit of happiness.

5. (Para. 9) That to secure these rights, governments are instituted among men, *deriving their just powers from the consent of the governed.*

Vocabulary Exercises

I. **Fill in each blank with one of the given words and note the difference of meaning between them. Change the form when necessary.**

1. ASSUMPTION   PRESUMPTION
   A. A lot of people make the _____ that poverty only exists in the under-developed countries.
   B. We are working on the project on the _____ that the fund will come through.
   C. Don't believe what he said. There is a strong _____ against the truthfulness of his statement.

2. STRETCH   PROLONG   EXTEND   LENGTHEN

   A. The Chinese delegation decided to _____ their visit in New York by one week.
   B. My blue sweater has _____ completely out of shape.
   C. The forest _____ in all directions as far as the eye could see.
   D. After a long day's work, she _____ herself out on the couch and fell asleep.
   E. The bank has promised to _____ our company credit.
   F. He wanted to have his coat _____ a bit.

II. **Choose a word or phrase that best completes each of the following sentences.**

   1. _____ Independence Day is the national holiday of the United States commemorating the signing of *the Declaration of Independence* by the Continental Congress on July 4, 1776, in Philadelphia, Pennsylvania.
      A. The   B. An   C. /   D. A
   2. My back has been bad _____ I fell and hurt it two years ago.
      A. ever after   B. for ever   C. as ever   D. ever since
   3. After all that killing, it's enough to be alive and well with someone _____ you love and trust.
      A. who   B. which   C. whom   D. as
   4. Around the year 1700, many _____ were fleeing their homeland to find an easier life in other European countries.
      A. German   B. Germen   C. Germans   D. American
   5. With a microscope, a whole new world of investigation _____.
      A. runs up   B. opens up   C. looks into D. runs out

III. **Fill in the blank in each sentence with a word or phrase taken from the box in its appropriate form.**

commemorate	interference	to begin with	obstinate
but for	in any case	wage	intolerance
as for	far-reaching		

   1. The invading Japanese troops met with _____ resistance by guerilla forces.
   2. A set of stamps has been printed in _____ of Independence Day.

158

3. _____ any further details relating to the author, the reader will receive satisfaction from the first pages of the book.

4. Jobs are hard to find but _____ that's not the problem because she has so much experience.

5. _____ in other people's relationships is always wrong.

6. Thus, the usual treatment strategy is _____ very low doses and to increase the dosage gradually as necessary.

7. His _____ insolence cost him many friends.

8. These new laws will have _____ benefits for all working women.

9. Does the President need Congress' permission to _____ war on another country?

10. _____ your help, I wouldn't have succeeded.

Translation Exercises

Translate each of the following sentences into English, using the word or phrase given in the brackets.

1. 在过去的几年里,她们为争取自由和更大的决策权而奋斗。(struggle for)

2. 昨天晚上我在看世界杯足球赛时外面的干扰声太大了,以至于我根本听不清解说。(interference)

3. 在我陷入困境的时候,他竭尽全力帮助我,我不知怎么才能报答他的好意。(in return for)

4. 你必须承认,你从来就没有全心全意地爱过她,而勉勉强强的爱还不如没有爱。(half-hearted)

5. 新的征税计划遭到强烈反对,这说明了现政府的无能。(opposition, incompetent)

6. 千里之行,始于足下,让我们从这个项目的最简单部分做起吧。(begin with)

7. 法院的判决将对医药行业产生深远影响。(far-reaching)

8. 她天生就有幽默感,因而我们都愿意和她交朋友。(be endowed with)

Text II

Father's Day

Pre-reading Questions

1. What do you think of Western festivals such as "Mother's Day" and "Father's Day?" Do you observe these festivals or not?
2. Do you think the Chinese have a similar festival to show respect and love to their parents? If yes, what is it?

1　　The origin of Father's Day represents a grassroots phenomenon that characterizes American reverence for the family. Although deeply rooted in North American social culture, the popularity—and, some might say, the commercial exploitativeness—of Father's Day has crossed national boundaries to become popular in other countries such as Canada and Britain. Americans and Canadians set aside the third Sunday in June as the day when children show their appreciation and gratitude for their fathers, but the earliest Father's Day celebration on record appears to have been held on July 5, 1908, in a church in Fairmont, West Virginia.

2　　Father's Day was first celebrated in local towns and cities scattered across America. The citizens of Vancouver, Washington claim to have been the first town to officially hold a Father's Day ceremony, beginning in 1912. In 1915, the president of the Uptown Lions Club in Chicago was hailed as the "Originator of Father's Day" when he suggested that the Lions hold a Father's Day celebration on the third Sunday in June of that year. The day was chosen as being closest to President Wilson's birthday.

Unit 10   Festival

3   Perhaps the most famous promoter of this holiday, though, was Sonora Smart Dodd of Spokane, Washington. Her inspiration for a Father's Day celebration came while she was listening to a Mother's Day sermon in 1909. Dodd wished to show appreciation to her own father because he had raised six children after her mother died in 1898. Her own father's birthday was June 5, so she petitioned the Spokane Ministerial Association to set aside that day in June of 1910 as a special day to honor fathers. The Association honored her request, but changed the date of the  celebration to June 19. On that day, the city of Spokane became the first city to honor fathers in this way, beating Vancouver's official claim by two years.

4   The governor of Washington took note of the celebration and declared that the entire state should observe the day as Father's Day. Newspapers around the country carried stories about Spokane's celebration of Father's Day, and the celebration soon received national recognition. In 1916, President Woodrow Wilson joined in a celebration of Father's Day by pressing a button in Washington D.C. which caused a flag to unroll in Spokane. In 1924, President Calvin Coolidge recommended that the third Sunday in June be set aside as "Father's Day" in all states.

5   In the following years, there were several attempts to pass a resolution in Congress declaring Father's Day an official holiday. In 1957, Senator Margaret Chase Smith attempted to pass such a resolution, arguing that it was the "most grievous insult imaginable" that Father's Day had not been recognized as an official holiday, despite the fact that Mother's Day had been celebrated as a national holiday since 1914. Finally, in 1972, President Nixon signed a law making Father's Day an official national holiday.

6   This holiday is marked by many interesting traditions. Roses are worn to honor Fathers: red for living fathers and white for those who have died. Many families celebrate the day by preparing the father's favorite meal, while children often buy special gifts for their fathers. The necktie is a perennial favorite, though power tools have become a popular choice in smaller towns, especially in the northern states. In larger cities, where a growing number of

employers allow casual dress at work, sports shirts have become a popular gift. Thus, the customs of Father's Day can be seen to have evolved to reflect social change. Over two thousand different Father's Day cards are available each year—less than the variety on offer for Mother's Day and Valentine's Day—but Father's Day cards hold the distinction of having the highest percentage of humor. Approximately 100 million of these cards are sold annually, compared to sales of around 150 million Mother's Day cards, but both are far outstripped by the almost 900 million Valentine's Day cards given each year.

7 Numerous churches continue the century-long tradition of recognizing fathers. Sermons often honor fathers and deliver encouragement to stronger family relationships. Indeed, for all the commercial and private family aspects of Father's Day, churches in America have remained the backbone of organized Father's Day celebrations, continuing to pay tribute to the work and dedication of fathers in a society that has seen many changes and convulsions in family life during the late twentieth century.

(728 words)

Reading Comprehension

I. **Answer the following questions with the information you got from the passage.**

1. What does "Father's Day" represent traditionally and currently?
2. Where was "Father's Day" first celebrated?
3. Who first promoted the festival—"Father's Day"? Why?
4. When was "Father's Day" declared as an official holiday? Who declared it?
5. How do people celebrate this holiday?

II. **Topics for discussion and reflection.**

1. Do you always show love or say, "I love you" to your father? Why or why not?
2. Please list Chinese and Western holidays. What holidays do you like most? Why?

Unit 10   Festival

Exercises for Integrated Skills

I. Dictation

Listen to the following passage. Altogether the passage will be read to you four times. During the first reading, which will be read at normal speed, listen and try to understand the meaning. For the second and third readings, the passage will be read sentence by sentence, or phrase by phrase, with intervals of 15 to 20 seconds. The last reading will be done at normal speed again and during this time you should check your work. You will then be given 2 minutes to check through your work once more.

_____
_____
_____
_____

II. Cloze

Fill in each blank in the passage below with a word taken from the box in its appropriate form.

practice	flame	popularize	customarily	commemorate
annually	attend	originate	date back	beforehand
consist	decorate	participate	attend	associate

Christmas is Britain's most popular holiday and is characterized by traditions which ___1___ hundreds of years. Many Christmas customs which ___2___ in Britain have been adopted in the United States and Canada.

The first ever Christmas card was posted in England in the 1840s and the ___3___ soon became an established part of the build-up to Christmas. Over a billion Christmas cards are now sent every year in the United Kingdom, many of them sold in ___4___ of charities.

Christmas ___5___ in general have even earlier origins. Holly, ivy and mistletoe (槲寄生) are ___6___ with rituals going back beyond the Dark Ages. The Christmas tree was ___7___ by Prince Albert, husband of Queen Victoria, who introduced one to the Royal Household in 1840. Since 1947, the country of Norway has presented Britain ___8___ with a large Christmas tree which stands in Trafalgar Square in ___9___ of Anglo-Norwegian cooperation during the Second World War.

Popular among children at Christmas time are pantomimes (童话剧), song and dance dramatizations of well-known fairy tales which encourage audience ___10___.

Christmas Day sees the opening of presents and many families ___11___ Christmas services at church. Christmas dinner ___12___ traditionally of a roast turkey, goose or chicken with stuffing and roast potatoes. Mince pies and Christmas pudding ___13___ with brandy, which might contain coins or lucky charms for children, follow this. (The pudding is usually prepared weeks ___14___ and is ___15___ stirred by each member of the family as a wish is made.) Later in the day, a Christmas cake may be served—a rich baked fruitcake with marzipan (杏仁蛋白软糖), icing and sugar frosting.

Oral Activities

Activity One: How do you celebrate Father's Day?

Although deeply rooted in North American social culture, the popularity of Father's Day or Mother's Day has crossed national boundaries to become popular in China. Have you ever celebrated Father's Day or Mother's Day? Discuss the ways to express the love for your parent in groups.

Activity Two: Father's Day cards competition

Each student is required to design a special card for Father's day and explain the meaning of the design to the class. The class will vote for the best design.

Activity Three: Debate: Should Chinese celebrate Western festivals?

Western festivals, such as Christmas Day and Valentine's Day, have enjoyed increasing popularity in China, especially among young people. Some people hold the opinion that Western festivals have greatly influenced the traditional Chinese culture

Unit 10 Festival

and people's way of thinking by cultural invasion. However, others believe that the acceptance of Western festivals can enrich Chinese culture and people's life. Which statement do you agree with? Should Chinese say no to the celebration of Western festivals?

Writing Practice

Note Writing: Giving information

A famous expert is coming to your university to give a lecture on Western culture next Tuesday evening. Everyone in your class is expected to participate. Write a note to inform your roommate, Jenny, who happened to be out when the news came. Write no more than 60 words.

```
                                              May ____
Dear Jenny,




                                              Yours,
                                              Emily
```

Passage Writing:

Why is Spring Festival so important to Chinese people? Explain the importance of the festival by introducing related customs, traditions, and how people celebrate it. You may write by referring to the following outline:

1. Spring Festival is a wonderful time of the year to spend with family.
2. Spring Festival is also a great time to visit friends.
3. However, there are times during Spring Festival when it is nice just to be by yourself.

You can also write about one of the other important festivals, such as Mid-Autumn Day, Qing Ming Festival, etc. Write about 120 words to introduce one of the traditional festivals.

Unit 11 Food

> **Warm-up Activities**
> 1. List all the food you know and describe the food to your partner.
> 2. Suppose you are a salesman for a food company, give a 2-minute presentation to promote your product.

Text I

How Americans Eat and Drink

> **Pre-reading Questions**
> 1. What do you think of American's eating styles? Can you name some American food or drinks?
> 2. Do you like American food? Why or why not?

1 Coca-Cola is the best-selling soft (non-alcoholic) drink in the world. 165 million "Cokes" are sold every day, from the equator to the Arctic. Whereas outside the USA Coke tends to be a young person's drink, inside the USA anybody of any age or income can drink it without embarrassment on any occasion.

2 Coke is not the only "cola" drink. Pepsi Cola is a well-known rival and has its devotees, for it is not as sweet as Coke. Cola drinks contain caffeine from the kola nut and are the only soft drinks which are stimulating as well as refreshing.

3 There are excellent wines produced in California which are praised by European connoisseurs, but some Americans prefer stronger stuff. Well-off Americans consume a lot of alcohol in the form of cocktails—mixtures based

on spirits like whisky, gin and vodka.

Hamburgers and hot dogs are perhaps the best known American foods. Hot dogs—sausages between bread rolls—can be bought in snack bars and from hot dog stands on street corners. And from San Francisco to New York, in cheap or medium-priced restaurants, hamburgers will be on all the menus, in company with steaks, fried chicken and seafood. They come with French fries and crisp green salad. In most cases it is certainly good value for money. For dessert you will be offered apple pie, cheese cake, chocolate layer cake, ice creams and ice cream sundaes. No ice cream in the world is more delicious than American ice cream.

The American passion for speed has now hit the food business. Many restaurants, in particular the great chain restaurant company, McDonalds, specialize in "fast-food", food which is served at the counter ready "to go" or "to take out". The food, cooked and hot, is packed into cardboard and plastic containers, and hot drinks go into plastic cups with tight-fitting lids. There are also drive-in fast-food restaurants, where the customer does not even have to leave his or her car. They first stop at a board where the menu is displayed, give an order through a microphone and then drive another twenty yards, where a girl hands them the meal, ready-cooked and packed. People who prefer to eat at a table in the restaurant also receive their food in cardboard or plastic containers, and the knives, forks and spoons are plastic, too. When they have finished, customers throw everything except the tray into a trash can.

In most cities, large and small, you can eat Mexican or Italian food. And even small towns have a coffee shop serving simple meals, drinks of all kinds, and excellent, freshly-made coffee. You sit at the counter, or are served at a table. Service in restaurants and coffee shops is efficient and friendly. Waiters and waitresses often introduce themselves, "Hi! I'm Don. What can I get you folks?" This friendliness is natural and not entirely influenced by the hope of a high tip. In any case, people usually tip 15% of the check. One of the pleasantest things about waiters and waitresses is that they refill your coffee cup several times for no extra charge.

7   Many American families pride themselves on their cooking, and have deep freezers, where they store food they grow in their gardens or buy in the supermarket. Supermarkets are large self-service stores selling every kind of food—fresh, canned or frozen. So, like the fast-food restaurants, their produce is less expensive and easier to market. There have been supermarkets in the USA since the 1930s, and they have now spread through a large part of the world.

(604 words)

Words and Expressions

equator	/ɪˈkweɪtə/	n.	an imaginary line drawn around the middle of the Earth that is exactly the same distance from the North Pole and the South Pole 赤道
devotee	/ˌdevəˈtiː/	n.	one who is ardently devoted to something; an enthusiast or advocate 爱好者
caffeine	/ˈkæfiːn/	n.	a bitter white alkaloid (生物碱) often derived from tea or coffee, used to make you feel more active 咖啡因
refresh	/rɪˈfreʃ/	vt.	to revive with or as if with rest, food, or drink; to give new vigor or spirit to 恢复精力 **refreshing** *adj.* 提神的
connoisseur	/ˌkɒnəˈsɜː/	n.	a person with expert knowledge or training, especially in the fine arts 专家（尤指艺术精品方面）
cocktail	/ˈkɒkteɪl/	n.	any of various mixed alcoholic drinks consisting usually of brandy, whiskey, vodka, or gin combined with fruit juices or other liquors and often served chilled 鸡尾酒（一种混合的酒精饮料，通常由白兰地、威士忌、伏特加或杜松子酒加果汁或其他汁组成，并通常使其冰冷后使用）
spirits	/ˈspɪrɪts/	n.	an alcoholic beverage (饮料), especially distilled (蒸馏过的) liquor 含酒精饮料，尤指非发酵的烈酒
sausage	/ˈsɒsɪdʒ/	n.	a small tube of skin filled with a mixture of meat, spices etc., eaten hot or cold after it has been cooked 香肠
snack	/snæk/	n.	a hurried or light meal 快餐

in company with			和……一起
French fries			long thin pieces of potato that has been cooked in hot oil 炸薯条,炸土豆片
crisp	/krɪsp/	*adj.*	pleasantly hard or firm when you bite it 脆的
dessert	/dɪˈzɜːt/	*n.*	a usually sweet course or dish, as of fruit, ice cream, or pastry, served at the end of a meal (饭后)甜点
sundae	/ˈsʌndeɪ/	*n.*	a dish of ice cream with a topping such as syrup(糖浆,果汁), fruits, nuts, or whipped cream 圣代冰淇淋(顶部有诸如糖浆、水果、干果或搅打起泡的奶油)
cardboard	/ˈkɑːdbɔːd/	*n.*	a stiff brown material like very thick paper, used especially for making boxes 纸板
container	/kənˈteɪnə/	*n.*	a carton, can, or jar, in which material is held or carried 容器
display	/dɪˈspleɪ/	*vt.*	to present or hold up to view, to show 呈现,展示
tray	/treɪ/	*n.*	a flat piece of plastic, metal, or wood, with raised edges, used for carrying things such as plates, food, etc. 托盘,盘子
trash	/træʃ/	*n.*	worthless or discarded material or objects; refuse or rubbish 垃圾

Reading Comprehension

I. **Decide which of the following best states the author's purpose of writing.**

   A. To persuade the reader to go to America to enjoy American food.
   B. To let the reader take a glance of the American people's food.
   C. To find out the reasons why American food is so popular.
   D. To introduce the development of American food.

II. Answer the following questions orally.

1. What does "soft drink" mean according to this text?
2. Who are the consumers of Coke outside the USA?
3. What are the two brands of Cola in the USA? What is the difference between the two products?
4. Which kind of wine do rich Americans prefer?
5. List the names of food that best illustrate typical American fast food.
6. How is American fast food served?

III. Judge: According to the text, whether the following statements are true or false.

1. Hamburgers appear in all kinds of restaurants in America.
   (   )
2. American ice cream is the best ice cream in the world.
   (   )
3. The American's love for efficiency is also reflected in their fast food.
   (   )
4. American people do not like food from other countries.
   (   )
5. American people do not cook food themselves at home very often.
   (   )

IV. Paraphrase, use your own words to explain the sentences in the text with the help of the context.

1. (Para. 4) In most cases it is certainly good value for money.

2. (Para. 5) The American passion for speed has now hit the food business.

3. (Para. 6) This friendliness is natural and not entirely influenced by the hope of a high tip.

Unit 11　Food

Vocabulary Exercises

I. **Fill in each blank with one of the two words from each pair and note the difference of meaning between them. Change the form when necessary.**

1. RIVAL   ADVERSARY
   A. Great Britain and Germany were _____ in the Second World War.
   B. Rose and Isabel are _____ for the tennis prize.
   C. Plastics have become _____ of many metals.
   D. Martin Luther King made many _____ in his nonviolent quest for equality.

2. DEVOTEE   ADVOCATE
   A. The leader of the organization stressed that she was not a(n) _____ of globalization.
   B. This judge is a strong _____ of prison reform.
   C. He is a great _____ of sports.
   D. _____ of jazz won't want to miss this!

3. DESSERT   DESERT
   A. Vast areas of land have become _____.
   B. I like to have ice cream for _____.
   C. If you make the main course, I'll make a _____.
   D. A soldier who _____ (his post) in time of war is punished severely.

4. DISPLAY   DEMOSTRATE
   A. The salesperson plugged in and _____ (how to use) the vacuum cleaner.
   B. The peacock _____ its fine tail feathers when it noticed any gay colours.
   C. Mr. Brown seemed to _____ no feelings when they told him the news.
   D. How do you _____ that the earth is round?

II. **Choose a word or phrase that best completes each of the following sentences.**

1. People under stress _____ express their full range of potential.
   A. tend to   B. are going to   C. are bound to   D. are to
2. _____ another occasion, he landed his helicopter in a deserted car park.

    A. In   B. On   C. Under   D. Upon

3. She prided herself _____ her ability to speak many foreign languages.

    A. in   B. at   C. for   D. upon

4. They want a house, _____ we would rather live in a flat.

    A. although   B. though   C. whereas   D. /

5. The arrival of the national football team _____ the headlines in the local newspaper.

    A. blew   B. hit   C. arrived   D. came to

III. Fill in the blank in each sentence with a word or phrase taken from the box in its appropriate form.

embarrass	stimulating	refreshing	stand
in company with	passion	special	middle
pack	friendly		

1. A cool drink _____ me after my long walk.
2. The travel agency next to my neighbor's company _____ in charter flights.
3. That man of _____ height is the professor who is going to preside over the special workshop.
4. When writing an argumentation, you should bear in mind that the interest of the reader must be _____ by the introduction.
5. Large _____ are sometimes left beside the door of the post office.
6. The decline of sales _____ the company.
7. Martin Luther King made a _____ speech against injustice to the black people.
8. The magazine usually sells out soon after it hits the _____.
9. Early the next morning the Mayor was walking in the square below _____ the Town Councilors.
10. Chains such as KFC, McDonald's and Pizza Hut are setting a new standard of customer service, using strict employee training and constant monitoring to ensure the _____ of frontline staff.

Unit 11 Food

Translation Exercises

Translate each of the following sentences into English, using the word or phrase given in the brackets.

1. 美国科学家历时 10 年所做的研究证明,女子往往比男子长寿。(tend to)

2. 实验证明,声音以波的形式传播。(in the form of)

3. 每当情人节来临,柜台上就摆放着五颜六色的情人节卡片,吸引了无数顾客。(display)

4. 欧盟宣布征税计划后,罢工浪潮席卷了众多西欧国家。(hit)

5. 她在攻读博士学位期间主攻澳大利亚文学,并出版了一本这方面的研究专著。(specialize)

6. 设计者没有料到,新公路的建成带来了交通量的激增。(come with)

Text II

Fast-food Fix

> *Pre-reading Question*
>
> Do you know the ingredients in fast-food? Do you think it healthy? Why or why not?

1   McDonalds announced this week that it was to begin printing nutritional facts on the packaging of its burgers and fries. The labels will include information about the fat, salt, calorie and carbohydrate content of its foods, currently available only on its website and in leaflets.

2   Clear, accurate food labelling is essential and, indeed, for some people, such as those with allergies or very specific nutritional needs, vital. Labelling lets consumers make choices about the food they eat: GM-free, organic, country of origin, etc.

3   But many people also say labelling is a key element in the control of obesity. The hope is that if the label tells you something is bad for you, you won't eat as much of it.

4   The Nutrition Labelling and Education Act of 1990 was a landmark piece of legislation in the US. Enforcement began in 1994, so for more than a decade Americans have had the most comprehensive food labelling system in the world. However, obesity rates in the US have continued to rise. So are Americans simply ignoring the labels?

5   A Cornell University study, which is going to be discussed at a conference in Washington next week, suggests that there is a big variation in "label effect" across gender and racial groups, with the only beneficial effect with regard to obesity being seen in white women. Yet this finding is likely to trigger a call for yet more labels. This is because of the belief that the rise in obesity must be due to the "off-label" habits of Americans—more than 40 per cent of the average American's diet consists of takeaway food or restaurant meals, which are exempt from labelling laws. Campaigners are now calling for these to be labelled, too.

6   Labelling is a fine source of information, but fat, sugar and calorie information tends to be accessed only when weight is already a problem, not before. And assimilating knowledge from labels while shopping requires dedication and an understanding of basic nutrition, which needs to be taught. This suggests that labelling is not the weight-loss panacea we believed it to be.

7   Perhaps psychology has a bigger part to play in our food choices. Chocolate-bar manufactures in Britain, for instance, have been surprised by the buoyant sales of steeply priced small bars of chocolate. We are prepared to pay more to eat less. So a more effective strategy of McDonald's might be to have a Small Mac Meal Deal with mini-fries and a skinny shake; same price, half the fat and calories.

8   Mind and food are inextricably linked. So it's good to see that the Foresight Project—launched this week to look at and help inform government policy on obesity—has psychology as a major strand. You never know, fooling us into eating less may be the way to svelteness.

(472 words)

Reading Comprehension

I. Answer the following questions with the information you got from the passage.
   1. What should be included in food labels?
   2. What roles do food labels play? Do you agree with these ideas?
   3. Why do people call for more labels?
   4. What tricks do businessmen apply when they persuade the obese people to buy their food?

II. Topics for discussion and reflection.
   1. If one wants to lose weight, what food should he/she take?
   2. What is the best way to keep fit or lose weight? Why?

Exercises for Integrated Skills

I. Dictation

   Listen to the following passage. Altogether the passage will be read to you four times. During the first reading, which will be read at normal speed, listen and try to understand the meaning. For the second and third readings, the passage will be read sentence by sentence, or phrase by phrase, with intervals of 15 to 20 seconds. The last reading will be done at normal speed again and during this time you should check your work. You will then be given 2 minutes to check through your work once more.

II. Cloze

Fill in each blank in the passage below with a word taken from the box in its appropriate form.

decrease	evidence	contribute	quantity	quality
benefit	risk	flow	publish	positive
suggest	consume	prevent	negative	compare
include	associate			

  Coffee is not usually thought of as healthy food, but a number of recent studies ___1___ that it can be a highly ___2___ drink. Researchers have found strong ___3___ that coffee reduces the ___4___ of several serious ailments, ___5___ diabetes, heart disease and cirrhosis of the liver.

  Among them is a systematic review of studies ___6___ last year in *The Journal of the American Medical Association*, which concluded that habitual coffee ___7___ was consistently ___8___ with a lower risk of Type 2 diabetes. Exactly why is not known, but the authors offered several explanations.

  Coffee contains antioxidants (抗氧化剂) that help control the cell damage that can ___9___ to the development of the disease.

  Larger ___10___ of coffee seem to be especially helpful in diabetes ___11___. In a report that combined statistical data from many studies, researchers found that people who drank four to six cups of coffee a day had a 28 percent reduced risk ___12___ with people who drank two or fewer. Those who drank more than six had a 35 percent risk reduction. But as the quantity increased, the benefit ___13___. At more than six cups a day, the risk was not significantly reduced.

  Still, some experts believe that coffee drinking, and particularly caffeine consumption, can have ___14___ health consequences. A study published in January in *The Journal of the American College of Cardiology*, for example, suggests that the amount of caffeine in two cups of coffee significantly decreases blood ___15___ to the heart, particularly during exercise at high altitude.

Unit 11 Food

Oral Activities

Activity One
Specialty Food Reviews in My Hometown

The students coming from the same province should get together in one group. After the group discussion, each group should introduce the specialty food in their hometown to other groups.

Activity Two
Work in groups and discuss the following questions.

a. What are your food likes and dislikes? From your perspective, what are food likes and dislikes related to?

b. Can you give some examples to show food likes and dislikes in the North and South of China? And in the West and the East? Try to explain the possible reasons.

Activity Three
Debate: Who is to blame for the rise in obesity?

With the fast tempo of modern life, fast food portions are getting larger and larger and so are the waistlines of many people and the diet-related health problems. Some people argue that fast food companies should take the major responsibility. However, others believe where there is a demand, there will be a supply. Individuals have the freedom and right to choose what they eat. If they choose to indulge in fattening fast food, they have no one to blame but themselves for the resulting weight gain.

From your perspective, who is to blame for the rise in obesity, fast food companies or individuals?

Writing Practice

Letter Writing: A Letter of Invitation

Write an informal letter to your friend, Mary, inviting her to a potluck dinner with you and stating your requirements.

23 March

Dear Mary,

With love,
John

Passage Writing:

Write an article about your classmates' eating habits in about 120 words, using the information from the oral activities. Both similarities and differences should be included in the composition.

Unit 12 Media

Warm-up Activity

What are the functions of media?

Text I

British Newspapers and Magazines

Pre-reading Question

Can you name some of the British newspapers and magazines?

1   The British are the most voracious newspaper readers in the world. They read newspapers at breakfast; they walk to the bus reading a newspaper; they read a newspaper on the bus, as they go to work; and on the way back home, after work, they are engrossed in an evening newspaper.

2   There are many 'morning papers', both national and provincial. The most famous is *The Times*. Contrary to what many foreigners believe, this is not a government newspaper. The various newspapers usually have their own views on politics, but they are not organs of the political parties, with the exception of the Communist *Morning Star*. The Labor Party and the Trades Union Congress no longer have a daily newspaper to represent them.

3   Bold headlines and a variety of photographs are features of the British press. Some newspapers, such as the sober *Daily Telegraph* and *The Times* (which belong to the 'quality press') use photographs sparingly. The more 'popular' newspapers, using the small or 'tabloid' format, such as the *Daily Express*, the *Daily Mail*, the *Daily Mirror* and the *Sun,* use pictures extensively

and also run strip cartoons and humorous drawings, some of which present striking pictorial comment on politics.

4   Besides offering features common to newspapers all over the world, British newspapers specialize in pages devoted to criticism of the arts and a woman's page. One feature found in many foreign newspapers is missing in British papers: the serial.

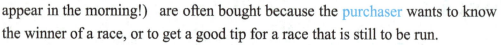

5   Nearly all papers pay special attention to the reporting of sport and athletics. The evening newspapers (the first editions of which appear in the morning!) are often bought because the purchaser wants to know the winner of a race, or to get a good tip for a race that is still to be run.

6   There is no censorship of the press in Britain (except in wartime), though of course all newspapers—like private persons—are responsible for what they publish, and can be sued for libel for publishing articles that go beyond the bounds of decency, or for 'contempt of court' (e.g. calling a man a murderer while he is still being tried). Such lawsuits are infrequent.

7   Besides the daily newspapers, there are a number of Sunday newspapers, many of which are connected with the 'dailies', though not run by the same editor and staff. The Sunday papers are larger than the daily papers and usually contain a greater proportion of articles concerned with comment and general information rather than news. The national daily and Sunday papers have enormous circulations (the largest in the world) running into several millions of readers in certain cases. The economics of newspaper publishing in Britain and in particular their reliance on advertising revenue have, in recent years, led to the closing-down of several newspapers; their circulations would have been considered large in many other countries, but they were insufficient to ensure the life of a national newspaper in Britain. Of the Sunday papers, the *Observer* and the *Sunday Times* are the best known; their literary and artistic reviews are particularly prized, especially among the more highbrow members of the community. Several Sunday newspapers now publish a magazine supplement in color.

Unit 12　Media

8　　　Some of the daily and the Sunday newspapers are at times criticized for being too sensational and devoting too much space to reporting murders and other crimes.

9　　　It is a regrettable fact that the number of magazines of a literary or political nature has declined since the war. This has probably been caused by the ever-wider use of radio and television. The most flourishing magazines are those published for women. Their covers are designed to catch the eye, and they certainly succeed in doing so! They offer their readers articles on cookery, fashion, needlework, knitting and many other matters of feminine interest. They also provide advice to those in love, 'your fate foretold by the stars', and stories of romance with handsome heroes. Some women's magazines also include serious articles of more general interest.

10　　　The visitor who looks at the magazines displayed in a large bookstore such as one may find in an important railway station will notice that there is a wide variety of technical or semi-technical publications. There are magazines for the motorist, the farmer, the gardener, the nurse, the wireless enthusiast, and many others.

11　　　There are many local and regional newspapers. It is customary in Britain for a newsagent to deliver the morning papers to his customers for a small extra payment; this service is usually performed by boys and girls who want to earn some pocket-money.

(756 words)

Words and Expressions

voracious	/vəˈreɪʃəs/	adj.	having an extremely strong desire to do or have a lot of something 贪婪的, 如饥似渴的
engross	/ɪnˈɡrəʊs/	vt.	to interest you so much that you do not notice anything else 吸引, 使全神贯注　**engrossed** adj. 被吸引的
contrary	/ˈkɒntrərɪ/	adj.	completely different and opposed to each other 相反的
sober	/ˈsəʊbə/	adj.	serious, and thinking or making you think carefully about things 审慎的, 稳重的

sparingly	/ˈspeərɪŋlɪ/	adv.	using or doing only a little of something 节约地，节俭地
tabloid	/ˈtæblɔɪd/	n.	a newspaper that has small pages, a lot of photographs, and stories mainly about sex, famous people etc. rather than serious news（版面比一般报纸小，配有大量插图，常以浓缩形式刊出耸人听闻内容的）通俗小报
strip cartoon			(BrE) a series of drawings inside a row of small boxes that tells a short story（报刊上的）连环漫画 **comic strip** (AmE)
pictorial	/pɪkˈtɔːrɪəl/	adj.	using or relating to paintings, drawings, or photographs 图示的
criticism	/ˈkrɪtɪsɪz(ə)m/	n.	writing which expresses judgments about the good or bad qualities of books, films, music, etc.（文学、艺术等的）批评，评论；评论文章
serial	/ˈsɪərɪəl/	n.	a story that is broadcast or printed in several separate parts on television, in a magazine, etc. 连续剧；连载故事
purchase	/ˈpɜːtʃəs/	vt.	to buy something 买 **purchaser** n. 购买者
censor	/ˈsensə/	vt.	to examine books, films, letters, etc. to remove anything that is considered offensive, morally harmful, or politically dangerous etc.（对书籍、电影、戏剧、信件等的）检查 **censorship** n. 书籍等的检查或其政策
sue	/sjuː/	vt.	to make a legal claim against someone, especially for money, because he/she has harmed you in some way 控告；提出诉讼
libel	/ˈlaɪbəl/	n.	when someone writes or prints untrue statements about someone so that other people could have a bad opinion of them 诽谤
decency	/ˈdiːsənsɪ/	n.	polite, honest, and moral behaviour and attitudes that show respect for other people 合宜；得体
contempt (of court)	/kənˈtempt/	n.	disobedience or disrespect towards a court of law（对法官、法庭等的）蔑视（罪）
proportion	/prəˈpɔːʃən/	n.	a part of a number or amount, considered in relation to the whole 部分
reliance	/rɪˈlaɪəns/	n.	being dependent on someone or something else 依靠

circulation	/ˌsɜːkjʊˈleɪʃən/	n.	the average number of copies of a newspaper or magazine that are usually sold each day, week, month etc. 发行量
insufficient	/ˌɪnsəˈfɪʃənt/	adj.	not enough, or not great enough 不足的, 不够的
highbrow	/ˈhaɪbraʊ/	adj.	being interested in serious or complicated ideas and subjects (被认为)文化修养(或趣味)很高雅的
supplement	/ˈsʌplɪmənt/	n.	an additional part at the end of a book, or a separate part of a newspaper, magazine, etc. (报纸或杂志的)增刊, 副刊
sensational	/senˈseɪʃənəl/	adj.	intended to interest, excite, or shock people—used in order to show disapproval 追求轰动效应的
flourish	/ˈflʌrɪʃ/	vi.	to develop well and be successful (事业)繁荣, 兴旺 **flourishing** adj. 繁荣的, 兴旺的
cookery	/ˈkʊkəri/	n.	(BrE) the art or skill of cooking 烹调术
feminine	/ˈfemɪnɪn/	adj.	having qualities that are considered to be typical of women, especially by being gentle, delicate, and pretty 女性的
fate	/feɪt/	n.	things that will happen to someone, especially unpleasant events 命运
foretell	/fɔːˈtel/	vt.	to say what will happen in the future, especially by using special magical powers 预言, 预测
enthusiast	/ɪnˈθjuːziæst/	n.	someone who is very interested in a particular activity or subject 热衷于……的人

Reading Comprehension

I. **Discussion: What is the writer's purpose in writing this article?**

II. **Judge: According to the text, whether the following statements are true or false. For false statements, write the facts in parentheses.**
   1. The British are known to be greedy.
      (   )
   2. Each newspaper usually has its own opinions on politics, representing a specific political party.
      (   )

3. Some newspapers use lots of pictures, while others do not.
   (   )
4. British newspapers offer a sports section, the serial and criticism of the arts.
   (   )
5. Both the daily newspapers and the Sunday papers specialize in news.
   (   )
6. Visitors to Britain can find many kinds of magazines that cater to different tastes.
   (   )

III. **Paraphrase, use your own words to explain the sentences in the text with the help of the context.**

1. (Para. 1) The British are the most voracious newspaper readers in the world.

2. (Para. 2) The various newspapers usually have their own views on politics, but they are not organs of the political parties, with the exception of the Communist *Morning Star*.

3. (Para. 6) There is no censorship of the press in Britain (except in wartime), though of course all newspapers—like private persons—are responsible for what they publish, and can be sued for libel for publishing articles that go beyond the bounds of decency, or for 'contempt of court' (e.g. calling a man a murderer while he is still being tried). Such lawsuits are infrequent.

4. (Para. 7) The Sunday papers are larger than the daily papers and usually contain a greater proportion of articles concerned with comment and general information rather than news.

5. (Para. 7) The economics of newspaper publishing in Britain and in particular their reliance on advertising revenue have, in recent years, led to the

closing-down of several newspapers; their circulations would have been considered large in many other countries, but they were insufficient to ensure the life of a national newspaper in Britain.

6. (Para. 7) Of the Sunday papers, the *Observer* and the *Sunday Times* are the best known; their literary and artistic reviews are particularly prized, especially among the more highbrow members of the community.

7. (Para. 11) It is customary in Britain for a newsagent to deliver the morning papers to his customers for a small extra payment; this service is usually performed by boys and girls who want to earn some pocket-money.

Vocabulary Exercises

I. **Fill in each blank with one of the given words and note the difference of meaning between them. Change the form when necessary.**

1. VARIOUS   VARIETY
   A. Those new _____ of wheat were the results of his hard research.
   B. The new style of shirts are available in _____ colors.
   C. There was little he could do to add _____ to his dull life.
   D. The party was cancelled for _____ reasons.

2. CONTRARY   CONTRAST
   A. He failed the examination, _____ to what I expected.
   B. There is a great _____ between good and evil.
   C. Your actions _____ sharply with your principles.
   D. Two _____ views emerged in the discussion on cloning.
   E. Kate was short and plump, in complete _____ to her mother who was tall and willowy.

3. BOUND BOUDARY BORDER   LIMIT
   A. The small town lies on the _____ between France and Belgium.
   B. There is no _____ to what you can do if you keep trying.
   C. We all have the right to express our ideas here as long as they remain within the _____ of common decency.

II. **Choose a word that best completes each of the following sentences.**

1. The government's actions are contrary _____ the public interest.
   A. of   B. to   C. against   D. off
2. She was suing doctors _____ negligence over the loss of her child.
   A. of   B. as   C. for   D. at
3. Rather _____ go straight on to university why not get some work experience first?
   A. then   B. than   C. with   D. to
4. The government is trying to promote long-term growth by reducing its reliance _____ income taxes that discourage savings and investment.
   A. on   B. at   C. with   D. off
5. Many schools devote almost one third of the allotted time for each lesson _____ these exercises.
   A. on   B. at   C. to   D. with

III. **Fill in the blank in each sentence with a word taken from the box in its appropriate form.**

voracious	represent	striking	censorship
infrequent	proportion	circulation	revenue
ensure	feminine		

1. Daily _____ for all of the nation's papers reached its peak in 1984, at 63.3 million.
2. The new law has been criticized by groups _____ disabled people.
3. All these ideas mean a huge loss of _____ to the Treasury, in the hundreds of billions of dollars.
4. Angry journalists accused the government of _____ of free speech.
5. The blossoms also signify the _____ characteristics of softness, mildness and peacefulness.
6. He has a _____ appetite for knowledge about what is happening around every corner in New York City.
7. From the outside, the most _____ aspect of the building is its tall, slender tower.
8. Roger's _____ letters home did not reveal much about his personal life.

9. The mobility of officials _____ that a variety of view-points are available for all districts.
10. A high _____ of the products tested were found to contain harmful chemicals.

Translation Exercises

Translate each of the following sentences into English, using the word or phrase given in the brackets.

1. 到了夏天,我就一直没有食欲。但今天游完泳后,我发现我的食欲大增。（voracious）

2. 牛顿全神贯注地在实验室工作,常常废寝忘食。（be engrossed）

3. 作为一名战士,他随时准备将自己的生命奉献给祖国。（devote to）

4. 在国民党统治时期,导演和制片人在电影检查十分严格的情况下拍片。（censorship）

5. 这位知名的女演员正以诽谤罪起诉数家通俗小报。（sue for libel）

6. 在贵国依照惯例是否应该付给服务员小费？（customary）

7. 很遗憾,我们失去了与贵公司合作的机会。（regrettable）

8. 空中小姐的职责是确保旅客的安全与舒适。（ensure）

Text II

The Formative Years of Sports Television

Pre-reading Questions

1. In addition to the excellent sports games, what else does TV broadcast during the games?
2. What kind of sports programs do you like on TV (sports news, live broadcast of the competition, or sports review, etc.)?

1   The game was played in Yankee Stadium on December 30, 1958. The favored New York Giants met the upstart Baltimore Colts for the championship of the National Football League. Many football experts claim it was "the greatest game ever played". Whether that bold assertion is correct is subject to further review, however, what is beyond question is that the game stands out as a turning point in the history of American sports because it established the NFL as a major professional sport, and revealed the vast potential the sport offered for commercial exploitation by television.

2   Even while commercial radio was in its infancy during the 1920s, scientists and engineers were already at work finding ways to transmit images over the airwaves. The first televised images were transmitted in England in 1926, and in 1936 an estimated 150,000 Germans witnessed the Summer Olympic Games in large halls in Berlin, Potsdam, and Leipzig. The following year, BBC telecast the Wimbledon men's finals between Don Budge and Frank Parker to some 3,000 British homes. Television in Germany and Great Britain moved forward more rapidly than in the United States because of government sponsorship and promotion. In the United States, decisions made at the end of the First World War had placed broadcasting in the hands of private commercial interests, and during the Great Depression even the largest electronics and broadcasting firms were cautious about investing in new technologies in an uncertain market. Nonetheless, television was on display in 1939 at the New York World's Fair, where 45 million visitors glimpsed the future on a nine-inch black-and-white screen.

3   During the 1939 baseball game televised from Ebbetts, viewers got a glimpse of things to come when Dodgers radio broadcaster Red Barber sat in the

upper deck near one of the cameras surrounded by fans as he announced the game. During one break between innings, he whipped out a box of Wheaties, filled a bowl, sliced up a banana, added milk, took a bite, and looked into the camera and proudly proclaimed, "Now, that's a Breakfast of Champions," That the future of American sports television was to be commercial-laden never seemed in doubt.

In the immediate postwar years, the Federal Communications Commission issued hundreds of licenses to local television stations and several manufacturers scrambled to produce receivers for the domestic market. For a time, the public was standoffish. Expensive and cantankerous, early television receivers were sources of both pride and immense frustration to their owners. By 1950, however, there were four million sets in operation that served 20 percent of the American population. In 1955, fully 75 percent of American homes were equipped with at least one set, a number that jumped to 90 percent in 1960. In that year, when voters elected John F. Kennedy president, more American families had television sets than indoor bathrooms.

As the preeminent professional sport, organized baseball was the first to take seriously the possible impact of television. After lengthy deliberation, its owners adopted a flawed policy that permitted each team to develop its own local radio and television markets and to keep the revenues thus generated. By 1960 the impact was already being felt; teams in large media markets were reaping far greater returns than those in small markets.

In 1953, CBS television launched the *Game of the Week* on Saturday afternoons. There had been network telecasts of the All-Star Game and the World Series for several years, but now regular-season games were made available. Fans everywhere could watch the top teams and such stars as Ted Williams for free!

The rest is history, as they say. Today sport's broadcasting is a 410-billion-dollar business, fueled not just by the "Breakfast of Champions", but by countless other major corporations that count on the popularity of sports and famous sports stars to popularize their products. Companies spend 32 billion dollars a year sponsoring sporting events through TV advertising. Television has brought sports into the homes of millions of Americans, and people all over the world, who would not have had access to live sports were it not for TV. Sports and TV have virtually gone hand-in-hand in making sports the important part of our culture that it is. It has made any and every sport available at the click of the remote control, and has made athletes into bigger-than-life heroes, some with world-wide followings. It is largely because of TV that sports are as popular and as lucrative as they are today.

(742 words)

Reading Comprehension

I. **Answer the following questions with the information you got from the passage.**
   1. Why was the football game between New York Giants and Baltimore Colts a turning point in the history of American sports?
   2. Why did Television in Germany and Great Britain move forward more rapidly than in the United States?
   3. What does the sentence mean, "Now, that's a Breakfast of Champions"?
   4. What sport was the first to take seriously the impact of television?
   5. What benefits can be obtained from sports broadcasting?

II. **Topics for discussion and reflection.**
   1. In what way do you always watch sports games (watching TV at home with your family, watching the live broadcast in a bar with many other sports fans, etc.)? Explain.
   2. Do you like advertisements during TV sports broadcasting? Explain.

Exercises for Integrated Skills

I. **Dictation**

   Listen to the following passage. Altogether the passage will be read to you four times. During the first reading, which will be read at normal speed, listen and try to understand the meaning. For the second and third readings, the passage will be read sentence by sentence, or phrase by phrase, with intervals of 15 to 20 seconds. The last reading will be done at normal speed again and during this time you should check your work. You will then be given 2 minutes to check through your work once more.

_____

_____

_____

_____

II. Cloze

Fill in each blank in the passage below with a word or phrase taken from the box in its appropriate form.

as a result	present	acknowledge	repeated
influential	harsh	consist	feature
competitive	interest	possible	come to
program			

The news media in the United States ___1___ of radio, television and newspapers. Together they are ___2___ on the lives of many Americans. Most Americans begin their day by reading the newspaper or watching a morning news ___3___. Throughout the day the news is broadcast ___4___ on the radio and television. In the evening news is a prime ___5___ on television with up to two hours of news in the early evening and more news late at night. For those who prefer reading, the evening newspapers offer them the ___6___ of reading the news.

The news media must ___7___ the public, and it is a big business. However, it is a very ___8___ business, because stations or papers compete with each other for listeners and readers. Each tries to ___9___ the latest news Americans want to know. When it ___10___ an item such as an election or war, all the news media will report the same thing. ___11___, listeners, viewers or readers might find it difficult to choose. Nevertheless, most Americans would not criticize their news media too ___12___. The credibility of the news media is generally ___13___ and accepted by the American public.

Oral Activities

Activity One

Survey and Report

Make a survey of English newspapers and magazines. Bring your favorite newspapers or magazines to class, summarize the features, and share the parts you enjoy most, present the reasons to your classmates.

Activity Two

Work in groups and discuss the following questions.

1. How do quality papers differ from the more popular papers?
2. How do newspapers and magazines influence people's thinking and behavior? Give reasons and specific examples to support your view.
3. What are the differences between traditional media and new media? Do you think new media is a great challenge to the traditional media?
4. As a type of new media, a blog is a platform for communication that can reach anyone via the Internet connections, offering an opportunity for the silent majority to speak. However, a blog can be a double-edged sword for social communication. What is your point of view? Discuss this phenomenon in groups and report to the rest of the class.

Writing Practice

Note Writing: Making Arrangements

The Welcome Party for the freshmen is going to be held on this Friday. As the chairman of the Students' Union, write a note to inform all the students of the related arrangements. You should write in about 60 words.

> September_____
>
> Dear all,
>
>
>
> Yours,
> Mary

Passage Writing:

Nowadays the media mainly consists of radio, television, newspapers, magazines, journals, and the Internet. Each type has its own advantages and disadvantages. How do you like each of them? Express your views in about 200 words.

References

Bulkeley, K. (2000) *Transforming Dreams: Learning Spiritual Lessons from the Dreams You Never Forget*. Malden, MA: John Wiley & Sons Inc.

Coolidge, F. (2006) *Dream Interpretation as a Psychotherapeutic Technique*. Oxon: Radcliffe Publishing Ltd.

Griffiths, C. (2003). Patterns of language learning strategy use. *System*, 31, 367-383.

Hardy, C., Burke, K., & Crace, R. (2004). Coaching: An effective Communication System. In S. Murphy, (Ed.), *The Sport Psych Handboo*k. Champaign, IL: Human Kinetics.

Mackenzie, M. & Westwood, L. (1983) *Background to Britain*. London: The Macmillan Press Ltd.

Musman, R. (1983) *Background to the U.S.A.* London: The Macmillan Press Ltd.

Nelson, R. & MacNee, M. (1994) *The Olympic Factbook—A Spectator's Guide to the Summer Games*. U.S.A. : Visible Ink Press.

Oxford, R. (1990). *Language Learning Strategies: What Every Teacher Should Know*. New York: Newbury House

Rubin, J. (1975). What the "good language learner" can teach us. *TESOL Quarterly*, 9/1, 41-51.

Russell, R. V. (2002) *Pastimes: The Context of Contemporary Leisure*. Champaign, IL: Sagamore Publishing, Inc.

Tiersky, E. & Tiersky, M. (1990) *The USA Customs and Institutions*. New York: Longman Publishing Group.

何兆熊.(2005)《综合教程》(新世纪高等院校英语专业本科生系列教材).上海:上海外语教育出版社.

田慧,朱珠.(2007)《体育英语报刊选读》.北京:北京大学出版社.

田慧,李晶.(2007)《走近奥运》.北京:北京体育大学出版社.

田慧.(2008)《现代英汉汉英体育大词典》.北京:人民体育出版社.

杨立民.(2002)《现代大学英语》学生用书第一册.北京:外语教学与研究出版社.

http://www.mindpub.com/art457.htm

http://www.intentblog.com/archives/2006/01/ten_keys_to_hap.html

http://searchwarp.com/swa21380.htm

http://www.ezinearticles.com

The Times